Under
ETHIOPIAN
Skies

D0943430

Ethiopian Tourist Trading Enterprise

The Authors

Graham Hancock, was formerly East Africa correspondent for *The Economist* and covered the Ogaden war between Somalia and Ethiopia for the London *Sunday Times*. As well as *Under Ethiopian Skies,* his books include *Journey through Pakistan* (with Mohamed Amin and Duncan Willetts), *African Ark: Peoples of the Horn, Lords of Poverty,* which earned the 1990 H L Menken Award, best sellers: *Keeper of Genesis, The Sign and the Seal* and *Fingerprints of Gods,* which by 1997 had sold more than three million copies around the world.

Dr Richard Pankhurst is currently a professor at the institute of Ethiopian Studies of Addis Ababa University. As well as *Under Ethiopian Skies,* his books include *The History of Ethiopian Towns, Economic History of Ethiopia, Social History of Ethiopia, Medical History of Ethiopia, Ethiopia Photographed* (with Denis Gerald) and *Ethiopia Engraved* (with Leila Ingramis).

Photography

Duncan Willetts, one of Africa and Europe's major creative photographers, was born in England in 1945. A regular contributor to *Timelife, Newsweek,* and other major magazines and newspapers around the world, his books with Mohamed Amin include *Journey through Pakistan, Journey through Kenya, Journey through Tanzania, Karachi, The Last of the Maasai, Railway across the Equator, Journey through Nepal, Lahore, Kenya: The Magic Land, Roof of the World, Journey through Zimbabwe, On God's Mountain: the story of Mount Kenya, Pakistan: From Mountains to Sea, Journey through Maldives, Journey through Namibia, Journey through Jordan, Journey through Seychelles and Spectrum Guides to African Wildlife Safaris, Kenya, Pakistan, Zimbabwe, Seychelles, Tanzania, Maldives, Namibia, Jordan, South Africa and Ethiopia.*

First published in 1983

Revised second edition 1987

Revised third edition 1997

This edition published 1997 by
Camerapix Publishers Limited
PO Box 45048
Nairobi, Kenya

Editing and Production: Brian Tetley and Rukhsana Haq

Design: Craig Dodd

Revised Layout: Calvin Mckenzie and Lilly Macharia

Printed in Singapore by UIC Printing and Packaging Pte Ltd

Colour separation by Universal Graphics Pte Ltd

ISBN 1 874041 89 X

Front cover: Twenty-three metres high, the tallest stele still standing at Axum was carved more than 2,000 years ago from a block of solid granite. The techniques by which it was quarried, transported and set into the ground defy interpretation by modern science.

Back cover: Like a jagged silver blade, the Blue Nile River cuts its way through steep, forested gorges in the Ethiopian highlands.

Title pages: Sunset over a cattle camp on the banks of the Baro River in Illubabor region, western Ethiopia. Cattle are highly prized by their owners.

Overleaf: Flat-topped peaks, deep gorges and sheer cliffsides give Ethiopia's Simien massif a special character not found in any other mountainous region of the world. A result of ancient volcanic outpourings and subsequent weathering and erosion, the natural formations of the Simiens have the power to entrance the visitor.

Contents

Chapter One · Origins

Ethiopia is an encyclopaedia of geology and geography open for all
to read under the intense blue of the African sky. More than this, it is a
living book in which the whole story of Man from his first beginnings
millions of years in the past, through all the stages of his evolution and
development, may be studied with awe and wonder. The traveller in
Ethiopia voyages in time as well as in space, for here the drama and
beauty of the present are illuminated in countless ways by the grandeur
and majesty of the past and, in a nation that is building itself anew,
by glimpses and intuitions of a noble future.

Ethiopia is old, old beyond all imaginings. Situated in the north-
eastern Horn of Africa, equidistant between the Equator and the Tropic
of Capricorn, its bedrock belongs to the earth's first continent — a
continent known by geologists as Gondwanaland, of which Africa forms
the largest intact remnant. The structures of this 600 million-year-old
world, made up of hard, massively folded pre-Cambrian crystalline
rock, have been covered over in many parts of Ethiopia by more recent
formations. Our world has fashioned and refashioned itself often over
the course of geological time, and there have been several periods —
millions of years long — in which Ethiopia was flooded by encroaching
seas. Each of these inundations deposited thick layers of new rock
atop the original structures, giving a fresh appearance to the land,
concealing its origins. In turn, however, the soft sedimentary cloak has
been subjected to other forces — the weathering fury of wind and rain.
These forces, where they were at their most intense, scattered and
carried away the marine sediments so that today, in the north-west of
Ethiopia, in the far west, and in parts of the south, Gondwanaland
stands once again exposed, glittering with the ineffable fire of ancient
minerals like gold and platinum.

During the Oligocene era of geological chronology (about 40 million
years ago) a massive upheaval of the earth shook and lifted the
Ethiopian landmass. The power of the blow, like a giant fist driving
upwards, opened deep faults in the crystalline bedrock and its overlying
sedimentary layers. Through these faults boiled a stew of white-hot lava
that slowly spread and cooled, eventually covering an area of at least
15,000 square kilometres. At the epicentre of this activity, in the north
of the country, the lava reached a thickness of about 3,000 metres before
the outpouring stopped. Subsequent erosion of this volcanic core has
produced many of the dramatic physical features by which modern
travellers in the highlands of Ethiopia have been entranced — deep
precipices and gorges, tall pinnacles of jagged rock, weird and withered
landscapes that seem without rhyme or reason to have been raked
horizontally and vertically by some gigantic plough. Nowhere are

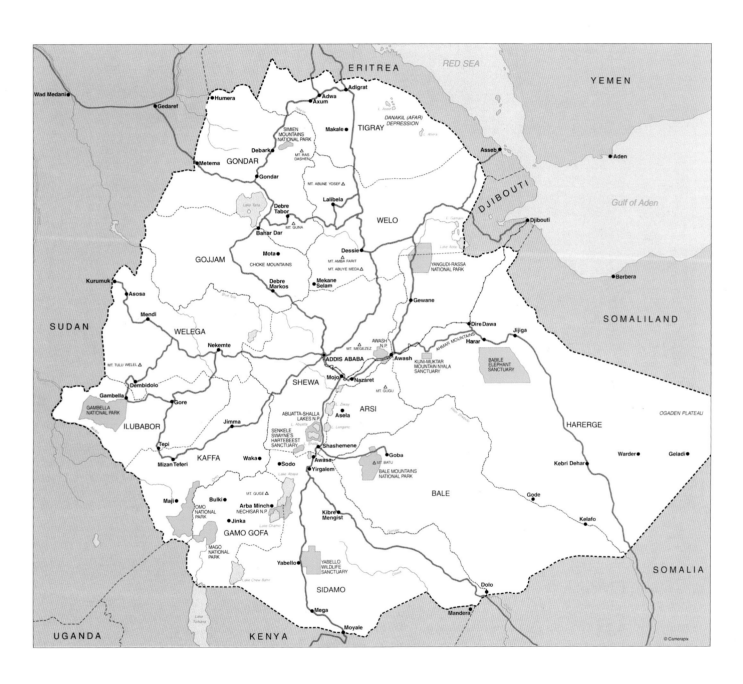

Below: Flamboyant trees, like scarlet sentinels, line the streets of many of the towns in the warm lowlands of the country.

these features more prominent, or more stunningly beautiful, than in the northern Simien region, one of Africa's major mountain massifs, of which Rosita Forbes wrote: "When the old gods reigned in Ethiopia they must have played chess with those stupendous crags, for we saw bishops' mitres cut in lapis lazuli, castles with the ruby of approaching sunset on their turrets, an emerald knight where the forest crept up onto the rock, and, far away, a king crowned with sapphires and guarded by a row of pawns."

The outpouring of lava that formed the Simiens contributed also to another major feature of the Ethiopian landscape. So much volcanic material was spewed forth that the earth's crust — lacking support from below — was weathered to the point where it eventually collapsed between two roughly parallel faults. The tumultuous subsidence that followed was part of a wider pattern that opened a massive wound in the surface of our world — the Great Rift Valley that extends nearly 6,000 kilometres from Syria, through the Red Sea, Ethiopia and East Africa, into Mozambique. It was at this time that the Arabian Peninsula,

Below: The Danakil desert, barren, severe and forbidding, presents a landscape that seems carved from the infernos of hell. Bleak reminders of the past furies that once ravaged this region, volcanic cones rise above the scabs of black lava.

geologically a part of Africa, was sundered from the rest of the continent. Scientists speculate that this process of sundering is still going on — gradually moving Arabia eastwards towards the Asian landmass and severing much of the Horn of Africa which one day, millions of years in the future, may form the basis of a major new continent.

Clearly visible from space to the first astronauts who walked on the moon, the Rift Valley forms one of Ethiopia's most remarkable sights, cutting through the country on a long axis that runs approximately north to south. The traveller journeying eastwards through the Ethiopian highlands will come upon it quite suddenly, finding himself confronted by an abrupt falling away of the land through diminished hillscapes to the valley floor — often more than 2,000 metres below. Following precipitous winding roads downwards, he will become acutely aware of the tremendous impact that altitude has on the climate and culture of this country. In the space of less than an hour's travel by car the clear invigorating air of the mountains gives way to the desiccating heat of the savannah and then desert; a long-established pattern of settled agriculture on tidy, regular fields gives way to the harsher realities of pastoral nomadism in a land where camels browse and fierce tribesmen jealously guard their cattle and water rights; alpine fauna and flora are replaced by scattered herds of plains game, stunted shrubs and gracefully spreading acacia thorn trees.

Extending inwards from the Red Sea coast the Rift is wide in the north, with the present Republic of Djibouti forming the approximate centre point. Here the volcanic floor forms the basis of one of the world's most hostile environments. In Eritrea, and in Ethiopia's Danakil Depression, there are many points more than 100 metres below sea-level where noon-time temperatures can soar above 50°C and where only the most specialised lifeforms can live. Immediately following the subsidence of the Rift, much of this area was flooded by the in-rushing waters of the Red Sea, a flood that was subsequently stemmed by fresh volcanic activity that raised barriers of basaltic lava. Behind these barriers the trapped inland sea that had formed began gradually to evaporate under the fierce heat of the sun — a process that is almost complete today. Only a few scattered, highly saline lakes — Gamarri, Affambo, Bario, and Abbe — remain. Elsewhere, as for example in the Dallol Depression, there are huge beds of natural salt which, at points, are calculated to be several thousands of metres thick. Here, too, amidst the yellow and reeking sulphur fields, alarming earth tremors are frequently felt, and there are several still-active volcanoes — dying reminders of the past furies that once ravaged this zone and bequeathed to it a burnt and ravaged landscape that seems carved from the infernos of hell.

Southwards down the Rift the basaltic lava floor and valley walls appear older, more weather-worn. Here, above the mid-point of the great Awash River, there is no current volcanic activity as such; but many fumaroles and hot-springs provide an indication of how thin and fragile the earth's surface still is in this region. Gradually the black and barren desert environment softens into savannah grasslands that provide ideal grazing for the wandering cattle herds of Ethiopia's nomadic pastoralists. And further south still, where the Rift narrows into a funnel between the main highland massif on the west and the mountains of Harar, Arssi, Bale and Sidamo to the east, the soil becomes sufficiently rich to permit farming.

This gradual transformation of the Rift's terrain has its origins in the quite recent geological past — the 'Ice Ages' of northern Europe which were, in Africa, characterised not by ice but by millennia of heavy rainfall. Since the last of the Pluvial Periods the climate of Africa has become progressively hotter and drier and this evaporating desiccating process has been at its most severe in the northern reaches of the Ethiopian Rift. Conversely, the central and parts of the southern sections of the Valley, more heavily inundated in the past, have suffered relatively less from the drying forces of the present, with the result that a long chain of seven large and beautiful lakes remain to delight the traveller in the heart of Ethiopia. Of this chain the northernmost is Lake Ziway, less than two hours' drive from Ethiopia's highland capital Addis Ababa. Southwards from here, three further lakes — Abyata, Shala and Langano — are clustered closely together, followed by Lake Awasa and, much further south, by Lakes Abaya and Chamo. Gazing on these lovely expanses of water today, one cannot help but speculate on the majesty that must once have been theirs when the great rains poured down over Africa. They are, according to one geographer, "but small puddles compared to their former size". Nevertheless, their shrinkage has had positive consequences, exposing huge areas of alluvial soil that allow prosperous and productive agriculture and creating a rich environment for wildlife and birds. Shala, probably the deepest lake in Africa north of the Equator, also contains the continent's most important breeding colony of Great White pelicans. Nearby Lake Abyata provides well stocked fishing grounds for these splendid birds and also excellent feeding conditions for many thousands of flamingos.

Ethiopia's geological past has played a crucial role in making the country today a vast and bountifully endowed natural haven for many kinds of wildlife and avifauna. More than 800 species of birds are found in Ethiopia, of which 26 are found exclusively in Ethiopia. There are also 103 separate mammal species, seven of which are endemic. The diversity of animals and birds owes its origins to the parallel diversity of the Ethiopian environment — mountains and plains, valleys and deserts, rivers and lakes. The existence of so many endemic creatures is due to the country's spectacular geological and geographic contrasts which have created numerous unique habitats and specialised ecological niches replicated nowhere else on earth.

In the scale of geological time, the opening up of the Great Rift Valley features rather a recent event — not older than 20 million years. Certainly it was the last massive movement of the earth to play any significant role in the sculpturing of the Ethiopian landmass as we know it today. Since then the terrain has undergone alteration — often dramatic alteration — as a result of isolated volcanic activity, of rainfall and of other erosional forces. But the truly gargantuan shifts of topography, environment and climate belong irrevocably to the far more distant past. In the quieter, more settled, more predictable

Opposite: Ethiopia is a land of birds with more than 830 species. Left: The Baglafecht weaver is recognisable by its yellow plumage, black mask and green mantle. Weavers build their nests in colonies and hundreds of the basket-like structures can be seen weighing down the branches of trees in Ethiopia's Rift Valley Lakes area.

Above: Carmine bee-eaters are perhaps the least shy bird of the plains; they are often seen sitting on the backs of cattle, game or even large birds like Kori bustards, waiting to catch the insects that are flushed out as their hosts move through the grass.

Left: The Abyssinian ground hornbill inhibits the open plains. It is a ground feeder usually seen in pairs or groups. Although a reluctant flyer, it makes a striking sight when it takes to the air.

and more congenial world of some 15 million years ago, many lifeforms began to emerge, bearing, for the first time significant resemblance to the lifeforms of today. Amongst all these, two in particular — monkeys and apes — hold a special fascination. Their story of struggle, survival, success and gradual evolution is very much our own story. It is a story in which Ethiopian plays a formative role as the land in which *Homo sapiens* first began to evolve as a distinct species from the apes. Here, Man was nurtured and allowed to grow before spreading out to east, west, north and south to colonise and conquer the globe.

To be recognised as the 'cradle of mankind' is a much sought-after cachet and, at one time or another, many countries have claimed the honour. Yet as palaeoanthropologists have delved deeper and deeper into prehistory it has slowly become clear from the painstakingly gathered evidence that Ethiopia was the home of Man's earliest ancestors. Nowhere else is the fossil record more vivid or complete; nowhere else have older recognisably man-like remains been found.

Until 1974, when the breathtaking discovery of an almost complete hominid skeleton at least 3.5 million years old was made at Hadar on the lower Awash River in Ethiopia's Danakil region, scientists had believed the shores of Lake Turkana in northern Kenya to be the cradle of mankind. Indeed, geologically and geographically, Turkana is very much part of the same zone as the Hadar site — both are situated in the boulder-strewn volcanic floor of the Great African Rift; the Kenyan lake is just that much further south. However, despite years of research by large teams of scientists led by Dr Richard Leakey, Turkana has yielded no hominid fossil older than two million years that is indisputably ancestral to modern man.

By far the most spectacular discovery made by Richard Leakey's team was a virtually intact human-like skull which has been dated accurately at a shade under two million years old. This skull, found at Koobi Fora on the western shore of Lake Turkana, has a brain capacity of some 775 cc — about 600 cc less than the brain capacity of modern man. It has been identified as belonging to a species dubbed by scientists as *Homo habilis* (literally 'Handy Man' or 'Tool-using Man'). From it a direct line of descent can be traced to a younger species with a still larger brain and even more recognisably human characteristics, *Homo erectus* — 'Upright-walking Man'. And from *erectus*, whose fossil remains date back at most 1.5 million years, it is not difficult to trace the lineage to our own species, *Homo sapiens* (literally 'Wise' or 'Knowing Man') — a species that, incidentally, is probably not much older than 100,000 years. Just a blink of the eye on the evolutionary time-scale.

There is very little dispute about the family tree connecting *Homo habilis* at two million years to *Homo sapiens* at 100,000 years. It is only when we look back deeper into time that the arguments — often very bitter arguments amongst palaeoanthropologists — begin. For many years however, there was a generally accepted belief that an earlier upright-walking, but otherwise ape-like creature (*Australopithecus africanus*, 'Southern Ape') was the earliest true ancestor of modern man.

This belief only began to be seriously challenged when it became clear that there were actually two types of *Australopithecinae* — a 'robust', specialised form with massive molar teeth, and a 'gracile', finely boned, less specialised form. The crux of the problem was that the gracile form, with fossils dating back 2.5 million years, was older by a good million years than the robust form; yet the gracile form, *Australopithecus africanus*, was, in every respect, far closer to *Homo* than the evolutionarily more recent *Australopithecus robustus*. How, scientists began to ask, could the *Australopithecinae* be ancestral to modern man when, as a group, they demonstrated a clear evolutionary trend all of their own from a gracile and non-specialised species to a robust and highly specialised species that lived on the earth at the same time — about 1.5 million years ago — as the far more advanced *Homo erectus*? Obviously there was something seriously wrong with the family trees that had been drawn up so far, and the search would have to begin for an older ancestor who was, perhaps, the progenitor of *both* the *Australopithecus* and the *Homo* lines.

It was this progenitor that was discovered at the Hadar site in Ethiopia, and it was a discovery that rocked the world of palaeo-anthropology by pushing back the ancestry of our species at least a million years further into the past.

The first fossil skeleton of this early ancestor unearthed at Hadar was dubbed 'Lucy' by its finder, Dr Donald Johanson of Cleveland University. The nickname came about because his radio was playing a popular tune 'Lucy in the Sky with Diamonds' at the time. It was appropriate because the skeleton is that of a female, and it is a name that has stuck in the popular imagination. The Ethiopians have called her *Dinqinesh* which simply means 'Thou art Wonderful'.

What exactly is Dinqinesh? Of this Johanson has no doubt. She is an ape but a very old, upright-walking, fully bipedal ape with teeth quite similar to those of 20th-century humans. When she lived she stood just a metre tall. She had a correspondingly small brain of around 380 cc, not much larger than that of a modern chimpanzee. "Here," as Johanson puts it, "was an ape-brained little creature with pelvis and leg bones almost identical in function with those of modern humans . . . Now I knew, with the certainty provided by this extraordinary fossil, that hominids had walked erect at three million BC."

After much further study, Johanson gave Dinqinesh a proper species name of her own, *Australopithecus afarensis* and, in doing so, redrew the family tree of humankind. Summarising her significance, he explains that Dinqinesh devastated at a stroke a long cherished belief of palaeoanthropologists that fully erect posture, a key indicator of 'humanness', evolved in tandem with that other decisive characteristic of humanity — a large brain. More than this, however, he and his colleagues have demonstrated that *Australopithecus afarensis* "represents a common ancestor to the later *Australopithecines* and to *Homo*; that the divergence between the latter two types probably began at around three million BC; and that *africanus* represents an intermediate stage on the way to *robustus*. We do not believe that it (*africanus*) was ancestral to humans. We believe that the emergence of human beings began sometime after three million years ago. By two million years ago it had been accomplished. By then, creatures recognisable as *Homo*

Left: Illuminated Bibles, hand-painted on parchment by priests and monks and bound within wooden covers, are still used in church services today. Often very ancient, they are written in Ge'ez, the language from which many of the present-day Ethiopian tongues are derived.

Islam came early to Ethiopia, and has since played an important and formative role in the life and culture of the country. Pictured below, one of the mosques of Harar, a city in eastern Ethiopia considered by many to be the fourth most holy centre of the Islamic world.

Opposite: Priests sing to a mournful drum rhythm at the monastery of Ura-Kidanemeret, Lake Tana. Music and dance are an integral part of the religious ceremony in the Ethiopian Orthodox Church, and their mastery requires many years of rigorous training. Yared, a sixth century Ethiopian saint, is said to have devised the first system of musical notation in Africa and to have composed the entire body of formalised sacred music and dance still in use in Ethiopia today.

walked on earth. So did their cousins the robust *Australopithecines*. For about a million years they appear to have walked side by side. By one million BC there were no *Australopithecines* left, they had all become extinct."

Dinqinesh is, in short, that fabulous treasure long sought by palaeo-anthropologists — the 'missing link' between apes and men. She teaches us much about ourselves and about our past and there is every reason to expect that her homeland — Ethiopia — can help us to understand even more about many things of which we are yet unsure. How, for example, did Dinqinesh and her kind evolve from the earlier apes of 10 or more million years ago — the *Ramapithecids* — which, despite their extreme primitiveness, had teeth that seemed to foreshadow the teeth of modern man? And how, exactly, did Dinqinesh, *Australopithecus afarensis*, evolve in her turn into the more human-like forms of two million and less years ago? The Rift, Johanson is sure, holds the answers to these questions: "Its bones will make Ethiopia the hominid-fossil centre of the world, with the entire story told there. We will have something between *Ramapithecid* apes and Lucy at around six million. We will have Lucy herself between four and three. Then we will have later *afarensis* types sliding off towards *Homo* in one direction and *africanus* in the other. Finally, we will have *erectus*."

Much remains to be done; to this end detailed palaeoanthropological work continues in the Awash Valley and, further down the Ethiopian section of the Rift, in the Omo Valley as well. Visitors to these bleak, sparsely-inhabited regions, travelling across the austere silence of savannah and desert, will find themselves imbued with a sense of awe and wonder as they cast their thoughts across the millennia to the survival struggles of our earliest ancestors — struggles to which we owe our place in the world.

The Ethiopia that Dinqinesh inhabited was certainly wetter, more humid, more densely forested than Ethiopia today, but its main physical features were the same — far to the east, extensive lowlands rising gradually into the cool mountains that now guard Harar and much of the modern province of Bale; then, moving westwards, the sudden plunge to the volcanic tumult of the Rift; then the steep ascent to the main highland massif at the north and centre of the country; and then, in the far west, falling away again to the plains of the Sudan. Most of Ethiopia's mighty river system — the Blue Nile, the Takezze, the Baro, the Omo, the Awash and the Wabi Shebelle — must have existed in Dinqinesh's time as they do now, pouring violently out of the uplands, carrying soil and silt to the thirsty deserts below.

In the midst of this wonderfully rich, diverse and beautiful environment, the story of modern man, of the first real Ethiopians, can begin to be read with some certainty only from about 12,000 years ago. The Stone-Age record is thin indeed, but Ethiopia seems, from the earliest times, to have been a melting-pot of peoples. There is much debate amongst scholars as to whether the two main ethnic components present in the country today — those speaking *Semitic* languages (such as the Amharas) and those speaking *Hamitic* languages (such as the Oromos) — were indigenous populations from the start, or whether they migrated to north-east Africa from elsewhere. Researchers are equally uncertain as to whether or not the Hamitic and Semitic races of Ethiopia had common or different places of origin. What is clear, however, is that 4,000 years ago, perhaps as a function of the divided nature of the Ethiopian topography, increasing linguistic and cultural specialisation and separation had become the order of the day. As sociologist Donald N Levine puts it: "By 2,000 BC, the proto-Ethiopians were beginning to separate into groups with different languages and cultures, a process that went on more or less continuously until very recent times and that was accelerated by the differential impact of external forces on indigenous cultures."

The first written records pertaining to Ethiopia date back to between 5,000 and 4,000 years ago, when this process of specialisation was just beginning. We owe these early historical commentaries to two of the most ancient centres of human civilisation — Persia and Egypt. It is clear that Ethiopia traded with both, supplying them with much-prized tropical products. Egyptian hieroglyphic records indicate that the Pharaohs obtained myrrh from Ethiopia as far back as 3,000 years before the birth of Christ. By the Fifth Dynasty we find King Sahure (c 2470 BC) despatching an expedition here in search of gold as well as fragrant gums and resins — which can still be found in the more arid sections of this geographically so varied country. Trade with India was likewise of great antiquity — Ethiopia has supplied the subcontinent with vast quantities of ivory since time immemorial.

Such ancient contacts provide the background for the rise, more than three millennia ago, of the pre-Axumite and Axumite civilisations which were located in what is now northern Ethiopia. Based on the capital city of Axum and the Red Sea port of Adulis, in what is now Eritrea, this area later emerged as the most powerful realm between Egypt and Persia, and enjoyed close trading relations with Egypt, as well as Arabia and India.

The achievements of the Axumites can be seen to this day — in the ruins of their cities and towns, with fine palaces and churches and noble obelisks, as well as reservoirs and dams — visible relics of a notable civilisation. The commercial development of Axum is likewise evident from the gold, silver and copper coins produced in the city — which are highly prized by numismatologists of modern times.

The Axumite kingdom, like the subsequent Ethiopian state, lay at the meeting point between Africa and Asia. The people of Axum, through living on the African continent, had close affinities not only with their neighbours to the west and south but also, across the Red Sea, with the inhabitants of South Arabia. The dominant sections of the people of Axum thus spoke a Semitic language, Ge'ez, sometimes also referred to as Ethiopic, which was related to the Sabaean of South Arabia, and hence, less directly, to Hebrew and Arabic. Ge'ez, which is written in a script derived from that of the Sabaeans, may be considered the Latin of Ethiopia. It is the language into which the Bible was translated, between the fourth and sixth centuries AD, and thus emerged as the language of the Ethiopian Orthodox Church. Ge'ez is just one of the many Semitic languages still spoken in Ethiopia

22

Below: At the Abol Experimental
School near Itang to the west of
Gambela, Nuer and Anuak,
children benefit from modern
teaching methods and an advanced
curriculum. Education in Ethiopia
has expanded dramatically in
recent years, reaching even the
most remote areas.

today. These include Amharic, the principal language of the present-day Ethiopian state and of modern Ethiopian literature; Tigrinya and Tigre, the vernaculars of the northern regions; the Gurage tongues spoken in a stretch of country south of Addis Ababa; and Harari or Adare, which is known only within the walls of the notable old city of Harar.

The Ethiopians, it should be emphasised, are the only people in Africa to have their own unique writing. The Amharic script, which is actually based on a syllabary, consists of 33 consonants each with seven different vowel-combinations, or a total of 231. There are in addition 20 symbols used to express diphthongs, as well as seven modifications of the letter 'b' to signify vowel variations of the sound 'v', which was traditionally unknown in Ethiopia but came into use in the 20th century when writing foreign words. Numerals are represented by special characters, partially derived from the Greek letters.

Axum, because of its antiquity and close contacts with both east and west, was involved at one time or another with no fewer than four of the world's religions: the Hellenistic faith of the ancient Greeks, whose Gods are honoured in the earliest Axumite inscription; as well as the three great monotheistic faiths, Judaism, Christianity and Islam. Each of these faiths, and in particular the latter two, has played its own formative role in building the culture and society of Ethiopia today.

Ethiopia, or more vaguely the land south of Egypt, was known to the ancient Greeks who gave its inhabitants their name — Ethiopians, or people with 'burnt faces'. In Book I of the *Iliad* Zeus is said to have departed for the country of the "blameless Ethiopians" — and a later text, the *Periplus of Erythraean Sea*, written early in the Christian era, describes the ruler of Axum as "acquainted with Greek literature".

Early Ethiopian ties with the Judaic world find expression in the legendary story of the Queen of Sheba's visit to King Solomon and the birth of their son Menilek, founder of an Ethiopian dynasty, as well as in the Ethiopian tradition, followed throughout the Middle Ages, of celebrating Saturday as the Sabbath. The country's historic ties with Judaism can also be seen in several present-day Ethiopian customs, including circumcision, the following of food prescriptions akin to those of the Jews, and in the presence of the Falashas, an Ethiopian sect following the Judaic religion.

The Axumite kingdom's conversion to Christianity makes Ethiopia one of the oldest Christian countries. Christianity, which became the official creed of the Axumite state early in the fourth century, during

Opposite: The statue in Addis
Ababa of Emperor Menilek II, whose
pioneering spirit contributed much
to the rise of the modern Ethiopian
state. Menilek was responsible for
the establishment of Addis Ababa
as well as for the introduction of
innovations such as piped water
and a railway.

24

Below: Agriculture provides the single largest source of employment in Ethiopia today. The temperate highlands of the country are a patchwork of fields that produce subsistence crops such as teff *(a grain related to millet) in addition to cash crops of coffee, cotton and oilseeds.*

Below right: Cheerful red cherries of Arabica coffee, Ethiopia's principal export, bagged prior to drying and hulling. Large state farms and cooperatives employing modern methods of cultivation and harvesting dominate the Ethiopian coffee industry today. However, bushes are cultivated on numerous smallholdings, and even grow wild still in some parts of the highlands.

Bottom: Zebu cattle, with distinctive lyre-shaped horns and humped backs, are seen throughout the lowlands of the country. In the cooler highlands experiments are being carried out in the husbandry of recently-introduced herds of dairy cattle.

Pages 26, 27 and 28 some of the many faces of Ethiopia, a land of great cultural strength and diversity.

the reign of King Ezana, had a deep impact. Most of the inhabitants of northern and central Ethiopia were greatly influenced by the teachings of Christ, though perhaps even more profoundly by the ideas and values of the Old Testament. Ethiopia became a land of innumerable churches and monasteries, as well as ecclesiastical schools, which for over a millennium formed the basis of its education and learning. Much of the people's creativity was directed to the composition of church music and poetry — a tradition still alive today — as well as to the painting of churches and the writing and illumination of precious manuscripts.

Islam also made its appearance early, indeed during the lifetime of the Prophet Muhammad. Some of his first and most respected disciples found refuge at Axum, for which reason he later commanded his followers to "leave the Abyssinians in peace" — thereby exempting them from the Holy War. Islam subsequently spread widely, particularly in the east of the country, though Muslims are today found throughout the land, and enjoy the same rights as persons of other faiths.

The Axumite state declined towards the end of the first millennium AD which witnessed the rise, further south in the mountainous province of Lasta, of the Zagwe dynasty. The most important ruler of this line of kings was Lalibela, who is reputed to have ordered the construction of the wonderful monolithic rock-hewn churches in the northern Ethiopian city which bears his name.

The centre of power subsequently again shifted south — in the late 13th century — to Shoa, the province in which the modern capital, Addis Ababa, was later situated. The ensuing Shoa-based medieval monarchy, whose rulers claimed descent from King Solomon and the Queen of Sheba, had many of the features associated with European feudalism, including a close relationship between State and Church. The Ethiopian monarchy had, however, no long-established or permanent capital, but relied instead on temporary military camps which were for the most part in or around Shoa. Several Christian rulers, among them the renowned Emperor Zara Yaqob, nevertheless travelled north to Axum for their coronation.

Culturally this was an important period in Ethiopian history, for the kings of this time, richer and more powerful than their pre-decessors, founded and endowed numerous churches. Several major literary works were composed in Ge'ez, while others were translated from Arabic and Coptic texts. It was in this period too that the Ethiopian royal chronicles — a major source for the study of the country's history — began to be written. These texts are virtually

Overleaf: St Mary's church at Axum. The first church of St Mary, dating back to the fourth century, was destroyed in the 16th century by Muslim invaders led by Ahmed Gragn. It was subsequently replaced by this battlemented structure constructed by Emperor Fasiladas in the early 17th century in the same style as his castle at Gondar. A third church of St Mary (and the only one open to women) was built nearby in the mid-1960s.

without parallel in Africa south of the Sahara. The medieval Ethiopian Christian state, which was far more isolated than its Axumite predecessor, appeared to Europeans of the Middle Ages as a land of mystery. It was often spoken of in wonder as the fabulous country of Prester John, the only Christian realm in Africa or Asia and, in the era of the Crusades, a potentially powerful ally of European Christendom in its conflict with Islam.

The Ethiopian state, which until then had never been defeated, suffered a major blow in the early 16th century. Ahmed Ibn Ibrahim El Ghazi, nicknamed Gragn, or the 'Left-handed', the Muslim ruler of Harar, making good use of firearms which were then beginning to be imported into the region, launched a successful rebellion and overran much of the country. Emperor Lebna Dengel thereupon appealed for help from the Portuguese who eventually landed a force of musketeers on his behalf and contributed decisively to Gragn's defeat and death in battle in 1543.

The conflict had however been detrimental to both contestants. Innumerable churches and monasteries had been destroyed by Gragn's forces, and at the end of the fighting the entire Ethiopian people, Christian as well as Muslim, were left seriously impoverished, while the victorious Ethiopian monarch, Galawdewos, the successor of Lebna Dengel, was faced with the difficulty of curtailing the ambitions of his erstwhile Portuguese allies. The borders of the Ethiopian state had moreover been rolled back, and what later came to be regarded

considerable interest to philatelists the world over. An equestrian statue of the victor of Adwa stands today, as it has for more than half a century, in front of Addis Ababa's cathedral of St George, a silent witness of the ceaselessly expanding modern metropolis Menilek founded just over a century ago.

The process of modernisation in Ethiopia continued slowly but surely after Menilek's death, despite the sad interruption of the Italian invasion in 1935. Italian occupation lasted until 1941 but was faced by continuous resistance and was brought to an end in the tumult of World War II by Ethiopian fighters and Allied forces.

The post-war years witnessed a gradual expansion of awareness among Ethiopians of their place in the modern world, and a growth of expectations of both individual and social rights. Throughout the 1960s it became increasingly apparent that the monarchical and essentially feudal system by which the country was governed, though doubtless appropriate to an earlier era, was no longer capable of living up to the aspirations of the people in the late 20th century.

In September 1974 Haile Selassie was toppled by a military council — the Derg — and eventually Mariam Haile Mengistu, one of the officers, became head of state, and Ethiopia fell into a state of civil war. Mengistu fled into exile in 1991 just before the fall of Addis Ababa.

After years of conflict, the new provisional government set about reshaping the country. One of the first outcomes of the new system was to grant Eritrea independence as a nation in its own right.

Ethiopia's main cash crops are coffee, oilseeds, cereals and cotton, with coffee pre-eminent, accounting for a giant 74 per cent of all exports. The Ethiopian climate provides an ideal environment for high-quality coffees (and, indeed, it is possible that coffee originated here — in Kaffa province, from which the drink is said to derive its name). Travellers through most of the central parts of the country will see much evidence of coffee cultivation, both on smallholdings and on large state farms.

Livestock is also very much in evidence, with Ethiopia's pastoral nomads still making a vital contribution to this sector. Large herds of hump-backed longhorn cattle, as well as camels, sheep and goats are amongst the colourful sights of many parts of the Rift Valley and also of the eastern lowlands. Ethiopia probably has more livestock than any other African country. The economic potential of the country is immense. With proper exploitation of available land Ethiopia could not only feed itself but could become a bread-basket for much of Africa. The potential of Ethiopia's, lakes and rivers is equally exciting.

Development of these resources could lead to a massive output of fish and fish products in the years ahead. The country's extensive river systems also hold forth another promise — that of virtually unlimited hydroelectric power. Harnessing of the mighty rivers that pour down off the high escarpment could produce an estimated 56 billion kilowatts of electricity a year; at present only two per cent of this potential is utilised. Yet electrification is proceeding rapidly. Visitors to Ethiopia Blue Nile Falls will see, as well as one of the most stunning and remarkable nature splendours that Africa has to offer, discreet signs of a major hydroelectric power station. From here the gleaming pylons carry current around the shores of Lake Tana to the city of Gondar and from there to the remote towns and villages of the high Simien Mountains.

Ethiopia's mineral resources, a product of the great age and giant transformation of its geological past, are another virtually untapped treasure. In addition to the gold and platinum trapped in its ancient crystalline pre-Cambrian rock formations, the country has much else to excite the attention of prospectors. Vast salt and potash deposits await productive exploitation in and around the Dallol Depression at the northern end of the Rift. The continuing volcanic activity in this region is also a sign of the immense potential for the generation of geothermal electric power from the many pockets of super-heated steam that are known to lie deep beneath the surface of the ground.

Perhaps one of the most attractive aspects of Ethiopia today is the way in which this drive towards modernisation harmonises with the traditional values of a rich and ancient culture. Here, one has the sense of a settled, mature community that will never lose sight of its own unique identity.

A mood of continuity links past to present, and present to future, suggesting that this country will take what it needs from technology, but will not allow itself to be overwhelmed by the technological ethos. Not so much a new society, therefore, but a very old one engaged in the adventure of rediscovering and reinterpreting itself, Ethiopia has about it a tranquillity and a certitude that are rare in the modern world.

Chapter Two · Mountain Stronghold

Ethiopia's northernmost state, Tigray, contains the first outposts of the high and mountainous escarpment in which this country's remarkable civilisation was born and nurtured. Towards the edge of this escarpment, the city of Axum emerged several centuries before the birth of Christ, as the capital of a state that traded with ancient Greece, Egypt and Asia. With its navies sailing as far afield as Ceylon, Axum later became the most important power between the Roman Empire and Persia and for a while, controlled parts of South Arabia.

The earliest records and legends date back at least 3,000 years. They suggest that it was from Axum that Makeda, the fabled Queen of Sheba, journeyed to visit King Solomon in Jerusalem and there, according to the First Book of Kings, "communed with him of all that was in her heart". In return, King Solomon "gave to the Queen of Sheba all her desire . . . So she turned and went to her own land, she and her servants. The Gospel of St Matthew in the New Testament similarly records how the Ethiopian Queen "came from the ends of the earth to hear the wisdom of Solomon".

Legend further has it that a son was born to the Queen from her union with Solomon. This son, Menilek I, the founder of the Solomonic dynasty, grew up in Ethiopia but travelled to Jerusalem as a young man where he spent several years before coming back to his own country with the fabled Ark of the Covenant which he and his companion had taken from the Temple. The Ark, according to Ethiopian belief, has remained in Axum ever since. Its present location is in a special chapel annexed to the church of St Mary of Zion. The Ark is in the care of an old and especially holy monk, and he is the only man who is allowed to see it — so historians and archaeologists are unable to test the veracity of the legend or penetrate the veil of mystery that surrounds the Old Testament relic. The present custodian inherited the honour of guarding the Ark from a long line of previous monks stretching far back into history; he is, with his dying words, supposed to nominate his successor who will, when his turn comes to die, nominate his own successor in this same time-honoured way.

Present-day Axum, a relatively small and lowly town surrounded by dry hills, does not, at first sight, show much sign of the splendours and pageantry of its past. Yet a closer look reveals that the modern dwellings perch above a vast part buried, part exposed archaeological site of incredible richness and wonder. Everywhere, the bones of long-gone eras protrude through the soil, adding substance to legends and bearing witness to the lost truths embedded in myths and fable.

Amidst this rubble of history the church complex of St Mary of Zion marks a rough centre-point from which the traveller can begin his exploration of Axum — an exploration that has much to reveal about the early origins of Ethiopian Christianity, a brand of the faith that is truer to its original forms and precepts than any branch of the historically more recent European Christendom.

The story of the Axumite state's conversion to Christianity is preserved in the writing of the fourth century Byzantine theologian Rufinus. He records that Meropius, a Christian merchant, or, as he calls him, a "philosopher of Tyre", once made a voyage to India, taking with him two boys whom he was educating in "humane studies". The elder was called Frumentius and the younger Aedesius. On their return journey the ship was seized off the African coast, apparently as a reprisal against the Eastern Roman Empire which had broken a treaty with the people of the area. Meropius was killed in the fighting. Rufinus states that the boys were found studying under a tree. They were taken to the king who made Aedesius his cup-bearer, and Frumentius whom he perceived to be sagacious and prudent, his treasurer and secretary. The two boys were thereafter held in great honour and affection by the king, who, however died shortly afterwards, leaving his widow and an infant son as his heir. The king had given the two Syrians their freedom, but the Queen begged them, with tears in her eyes, to help her until her son came of age. She asked in particular for the help of Frumentius, for his brother, though loyal and honest at heart, was simple.

Frumentius is said to have sought out such foreign traders as were Christians, and urged them "to establish conventicles in various places to which they might resort for prayer". He also provided them with "whatever was needed, supplying sites for buildings and in every way promoting the growth of the seed of Christianity in the country".

When the young heir ascended the throne, Aedesius returned to Tyre, while Frumentius journeyed to Alexandria, then a great centre of Christianity, where he informed Patriarch Athanasius of the work so far accomplished for the faith in Ethiopia. The young man begged the ecclesiastical leader "to look for some worthy man to send as bishop over the many Christians already congregated". Athanasius, having carefully weighed and considered the words of Frumentius, declared in a council of priests "What other man shall we find in whom the Spirit of God is as in thee who can accomplish these things?" He therefore "consecrated him and bade him return in the Grace of God whence he came". Frumentius accordingly returned as Ethiopia's first Christian bishop.

"These facts," Rufinus says, "I know, not from vulgar report, but from the mouth of Aedesius himself, who had been the companion of Frumentius and was later made a priest in Tyre."

This account of the Axumite conversion to Christianity — on any

Below left: The ground floor of the chapel adjacent to St Mary's church, which is said to contain the original Ark of the Covenant, also houses many other priceless treasures, amongst them the crowns of several emperors and of Frumentius, the first bishop of Ethiopia. Pictured here is the crown of Emperor Menilek II on the left, and that of Emperor Yohannes IV on the right.

showing one of the great turning points in the country's history — is accepted by Ethiopian tradition. The Axumite ruler who adopted Christianity as the state religion is believed to have been King Ezana, whose name is found on several inscriptions and different types of coin, some suggesting that he was a pagan, and others — presumably after the coming of the new religion — that he was a Christian. This monarch is generally remembered in Ethiopia by his apparent baptismal name Abraha, literally 'He who illuminated', while his brother Shaizana, mentioned in one of the inscriptions, is referred to as Atsbeha, or 'He who brought the dawn', and Frumentius, no less appropriately, as Abba Salama, or 'Father of Peace'.

Christianity appears to have spread rapidly in the Axumite realm, and early in the sixth century a Graeco-Egyptian traveller, Cosmas Indicopleustes, reported that "everywhere" there were "churches of the Christians" where the Gospel of Christ was proclaimed.

The oldest by far of these churches and, indeed the oldest church in Africa south of the Sahara, is the original St Mary of Zion, which dates

Below: The interior walls and pillars of the 17th century church of St Mary are decorated with many beautiful murals; amongst these is one depicting the story of the life of St Mary and another that of the Crucifixion and the Resurrection of Christ. Aimed at unsophisticated country folk, these paintings convey their messages with simple but vivid clarity.

back probably to the fourth century. Burned down 1,200 years later by the Muslim conqueror Ahmed Gragn, its imposing ruins still remain, spread over an area of many hectares, and have about them an atmosphere of mysterious tranquillity that has the capacity to entrance even the most rational and objective of visitors.

This ancient place of worship, because of its great age and its association with the Ark of the Covenant, was long considered the most important church in the whole of Christian Ethiopia. It remained the spiritual capital of the Ethiopian realm long after the decline of the Axumite state and many emperors who had made their capitals elsewhere in the country continued to journey to it for formal coronation.

One such ruler was the great Emperor Zara Yaqob who travelled to Axum early in his reign, in 1436, when, according to his chronicle, all the inhabitants of the city including its many priests, received him with great joy. This was perhaps scarcely surprising for he is said to have distributed 150 ounces of gold which he scattered on the carpets laid out for him to walk on, after which he sat for the coronation ceremony on an ancient stone throne, his 12 principal judges seated behind him, likewise on stone chairs, six on his right and six on his left. During his stay in the city Zara Yaqob granted the church a number of land charters, one of which stated his hope that it would serve as his "conductor to the Kingdom of Heaven".

The church of St Mary greatly impressed the 16th century Portuguese traveller Francisco Alvares, the only foreigner to describe it. He calls it a "very noble church" and "very large", with "five good aisles of good width and great length, vaulted above". These vaults were "closed at the top", and the ceiling and walls painted over. The "body of the church" was "well worked with handsome cut stone." It had "seven chapels, all with their backs to the east, and their altars well ornamented." The church was set in a "large enclosure" which was "surrounded by another large enclosure, like the wall of a large town or city." And within this latter enclosure were "handsome habitations of terraced buildings, and all spout out their water by strong figures of lions and dogs of stone", i.e. gargoyles.

After the destruction of this wonderful building by the forces of Ahmed Gragn, work was soon in progress — late in the 16th century — on a new church also dedicated to St Mary. Reconstruction was begun by Emperor Sartsa Dengel, but the building was completed by Emperor Fasiladas, the founder of Gondar. The present church is therefore crenellated in typical Gondarine style. Fragments of sculpture from the ancient church have, however, been built into the walls of its successor. The crowns of a succession of Ethiopian monarchs have been preserved

in the church treasury which also houses many rich embroideries as well as important Ethiopian manuscripts.

New St Mary's, as the Fasiladas construction is known to the citizens of Axum today, is still a place of active worship and its hushed interior, resplendent with many beautiful murals and paintings, evokes a mood of quiet contemplation. New though it is, however, it was joined in the mid-1960s by a yet newer St Mary's — an imposing modern cathedral with a huge domed roof which stands on an adjacent site and which, unlike the Fasiladas church, is open to women as well as to men.

Together, the three churches of St Mary constitute a remarkable testament to the continuity of faith in Ethiopia since the very beginnings of the Christian era. It is fascinating to recall, however, that Axum, the cradle of Ethiopian Christendom, also played a fundamental role in the evolution of the world's other great monotheistic religion, Islam — a role that is perhaps best symbolised today in the easy tolerance that exists between Ethiopian Christians and Ethiopian Muslims, who constitute approximately 35 per cent of the country's population.

When, early in his career in AD 615, his followers were being persecuted in Arabia, the Prophet Muhammad, according to Muslim tradition, pointed towards the Axumite realm and said to his disciples: "Yonder lieth a country wherein no one is wronged: a land of righteousness. Depart thither; and remain until it pleaseth the Lord to open your way before you." Many of the Prophet's followers, led by his cousin Jafar bin Abi Talib, therefore made their way to Axum.

Their persecutors duly followed them to the Axumite capital where they asked the then ruler, King Armah, to return them to Arabia. After interviewing Jafar, however the king refused, declaring "If you were to offer me a mountain of gold I would not give up these people who have taken refuge with me".

One of the refugees was Umm Habibah who later married the Prophet. King Armah himself performed the betrothal ceremony and gave Umm Habibah a dowry of 40 dinars of gold. On returning to Arabia she told Muhammad of the beauty of the great Ethiopian cathedral of St Mary at Axum, and of the wonderful pictures on its walls.

The Prophet, though he never visited Axum, was full of admiration for its people. On learning of Armah's death he prayed for him, and commanded his followers to "leave the Abyssinians in peace" — a command that, in subsequent centuries, they did not always obey. Muhammad, like the early refugees, was deeply influenced by this Axumite interlude. It is significant that the *Quran* contains a number of words borrowed from Ge'ez, or Ethiopic: such as *mashaf*, a book; *hawari*, an apostle; and *injil*, revelation.

In addition to the old St Mary of Zion, there are many other relics and remains in Axum dating back to pre-Christian and early Christian times. Amongst these, a series of inscriptions on stone tablets have proved to be of immense importance to historians of the ancient world. These inscriptions include a trilingual text from the early fourth century AD. Carved on a large stone slab by the order of King Ezana it is written in Greek, then the international language of much of the Middle East, Sabaean, the language of South Arabia, and Ge'ez, or Ethiopic, the classical language of ancient Ethiopia. This notable inscription — a kind of Ethiopian 'Rosetta Stone' — tells how Ezana, who claimed to rule parts of South Arabia as well as extensive territories in Africa, sent his brothers, Shaizana and Hadefan, against the Bega tribes to the north who had rebelled against him. These brothers captured six chiefs whom they brought to Axum, together with their men, women and children — 4,000 people in all, 3,112 cattle, 6,224 sheep, and innumerable pack animals. During the journey which lasted four months, these prisoners were allowed rations of food and drink, "to the full according to their number", including 22,000 loaves a day, as well as meat, water, wine and beer. On their arrival at Axum they were given food and clothing in plenty. The six chiefs were then dressed and decorated according to their rank, and were afterwards despatched to a region called Duala Baizen, the location of which is obscure, where they were supplied with a further 25,140 cattle. Obviously pleased with this operation, Ezana concludes his record by noting that he had erected at Axum five statues, one of gold, one of silver and three of copper. Several other inscriptions, also erected by Ezana, tell of expeditions in other parts of the country. Often couched in language which we would now term political propaganda, one text states that the king embarked on an expedition against a chief guilty of treachery; another tells of a campaign against bandits who had attacked and massacred a commercial caravan; a third tells of the king receiving homage and gifts from a people to whom he gave laws and regulations.

Yet another inscription, which is of considerable historical interest in that it reveals the king's conversion to the Christian faith, records how Ezana marched against the Noba, or Nubians, i.e. the inhabitants of the Sudan, who had rebelled against the rule of Axum "and made boast about it", declaring that the army of Axum could never cross the Takezze River to punish them. They had, according to the inscription, broken the peace, attacked and robbed their neighbours and stripped bare the messengers whom Ezana had sent to enquire into these matters. "I had sent warnings to them," he declares, "but they would not harken to me; they refused to cease their evil deeds and heaped abuse upon me and then betook themselves to flight." He therefore marched against them, and defeated them, after which his soldiers burnt their towns of brick and reeds, destroyed their temples and cotton plantations, and seized their copper, iron and brass. The inscription ends with Ezana's pledge: "I will rule the people with righteousness and justice, and will not oppress them, and may they preserve this Throne which I have set up for the Lord of Heaven."

Like the inscriptions, Axumite coins constitute another remarkable form of record and have done much to illuminate understanding of Ethiopia's past. The Axumite state issued its own currency from around the third century AD to perhaps the ninth or 10th century. During that time over 500 different types of coins were struck, over 170 in gold, 18 in silver, and more than 320 in bronze. Many, including some of the first, were inscribed in Greek, while others were in the country's classical language, Ge'ez.

The inscriptions on the coins are limited to the name of the ruler who issued them, his title, such as "King of the Axumites", occasionally the name of his father and, more rarely, the race or dynasty from which he was descended. There are also, particularly in later times, slogans or legends, such as "may it please the people", "by the Grace of God", "he will conquer with Christ", or "Christ is still with us". Some of the earlier coins, issued before the Axumite realm's conversion to Christianity in the early fourth century, bear the representation of the sun and moon — motifs also popular in South Arabia at that time, while subsequent ones are decorated with the cross, the symbol of

Christianity. Vast numbers of coins must have been minted at Axum. Each year many of them are unearthed, as was reported at the end of the 19th century by the British traveller, A B Wylde who stated: "After every heavy downpour of rain, old coins are washed out of the soil, and after one exceedingly heavy storm I was lucky enough to get two copper coins and a little bronze figure. The small Abyssinian boys are delighted to accompany a stranger about the place, and I have always had several to accompany me in my walks; they are intelligent, sharp-eyed little urchins, and take a great interest in the search for curiosities."

Wylde's observations are still valid today, and visitors who search diligently in the broken stony soil around the town can still unearth remarkable finds. The "sharp-eyed little urchins" have not changed either, and make pleasant and helpful companions on walks around Axum.

Neither are coins the only treasures that the earth conceals. Archaeological research in and around the ancient city has unearthed a great variety of other materials. These include statues, bowls and other

Opposite: The tallest Axumite stele, which according to local legend crashed to the ground and broke up in 850 AD, was 33 metres high and represented a tall and slender building of 13 storeys. With its rows of windows, and door complete with an imaginary knocker and lock, this symbolic house is though to have been regarded by its builders as a dwelling of the spirits of the dead. Alternatively, it may have marked the tomb of an important monarch of ancient times.

articles of stone, many kinds of pottery, both local and imported, as well as pottery heads, various glass bottles, jars and phials, a multitude of glass beads, a large number of bronze objects, including figurines and animals, plaques, some of them inlaid with glass, and sundry tools and objects of practical use, among them knives, spear-heads, tweezers, axes, cramps for fixing stones, many nails, a heavy hammer made entirely of iron, and a few fragments of mother-of-pearl and leather. Because of this wealth of artifacts, Axum has long been a site of major historical and archaeological interest. A British envoy, Henry Salt, conducted initial exploratory work here as early as 1805. His findings were later described, together with other antiquities, by his late 19th century compatriot, Theodore Bent, author of a classic travel book aptly entitled *The Sacred City of the Ethiopians* (London, 1893).

Modern archaeological research at Axum began with the German expedition of 1905-10, the findings of which were published by Enno Littmann in his large four volume *Deutsche Axum-Expedition*, which appeared in Berlin in 1912. This invaluable work contains numerous drawings, including 'reconstructions' of Axumite buildings, by Daniel Krencker. Axum's Red Sea port of Adulis (to the south of modern Massawa in what is now Eritrea) had meanwhile been investigated by an Italian scholar, R Paribeni, two of whose compatriots, A Anzani and C Conti Rossini, later studied the coins of Axum, while a third, V Monneret de Villard, subsequently published a further study of the city's antiquities in his book *Aksum, Ricerche di topografia generale* (Rome, 1937). Further excavations in and around the city were carried out, in the early 1950s and later, by the Archaeological Section of the Ethiopian Government, subsequently renamed the Ethiopian Archaeological Institute. This institution runs an important museum in Addis Ababa, where many artifacts from Axum including coins, are displayed.

The Institute also publishes its own scholarly journal *Annales d'Ethiopie*. In the early 1970s two French scholars attached to the Institute, Francis Anfray and Roger Schneider, published texts of several newly discovered Axumite inscriptions.

The oldest buildings, dating from the pre-Christian era, await further excavation before their origin can be confirmed. One such occupies an imposing site on the right of the Gondar road, about one kilometre to the north of the town. Here archaeologists have unearthed the remains of what was once a massive palace with finely mortared stone walls, deep foundations and its own impressive drainage system. The floor of a large throne-room has been discovered intact and, although the upper storeys and roof have long since fallen in, it is not difficult to imagine the rulers of ancient Axum holding court there. There are also private bathing areas of sophisticated design and there is a well preserved kitchen dominated by two huge brick ovens. Local legend has it that this palace was the original seat of the Queen of Sheba. In a large field on the other side of the Gondar road, facing the palace, there are a number of rough-hewn granite slabs, some standing, some fallen, among them a giant stele said to be the Queen of Sheba's burial place. Amongst these arcane memorials farmers plough the soil and grow their crops, apparently oblivious of the history on which they tread.

The stelae to the north of the town, perhaps 3,000 years old, are early examples of an art-form that came into its own in Ethiopia around the time of the birth of Christ and that flourished until the fourth century AD. Although found in all parts of Axum, the obelisks achieve their peak of perfection on a pleasant grassy site near the churches of St Mary of Zion. Here, amongst a number of plainer stelae, there are also three finely carved monuments which, because of their size and the intricacy of their beautifully proportioned execution, astonish the beholder. Only one of these amazing monuments is still standing, although another — looted during the Italian occupation of Ethiopia — can be seen in Rome, facing the headquarters of the United Nations Food and Agriculture Organisation.

The standing obelisk at Axum rises to a height of over 23 metres, and is exquisitely carved to represent a nine-storey building in the fashion of the 'tower-houses' of South Arabia. The front elevation of this lovely and impressive stele tapers gradually to the summit and is crowned by a semi-circular headpiece which some authorities believe to have represented the sun. The main decoration, on the front elevation, is provided by the semblance of windows and of beams of timber supposedly inserted horizontally into the walls, with a row of imaginary log-ends slotted into them as supports. The house-like appearance is enhanced by the presence, at the base of the monument, of a symbolic door, surmounted by a row of rectangular windows, somewhat smaller than those on the eight storeys above. An additional, and very successful, decorative feature is provided by a shallow central recess which extends, on the front elevation, from the base to the summit.

The architectural decoration on the front of the obelisk is carried out also on both sides, with suitable modifications. The back is, however, undecorated, except for a circle carved in relief near the apex, with the representation of four balls grouped together in the centre, and a fifth touching the circle's edge.

An altar, probably intended for sacrifices, is fitted to the base of the front of the stele. This altar, which contains four circular bowls sunk in its surface, is decorated with a border of vine leaves. Such altars are to be found associated with the other stelae. This remarkable obelisk has over the centuries impressed a succession of foreign travellers, among them the British envoy, Henry Salt, who wrote in 1805: "My attention was for a long time riveted on this beautiful and extraordinary monument." On visiting it half a decade later he observed that it "made nearly as forcible an impression" on his mind as the first moment he had beheld it. Explaining that he considered this stele "the most admirable and perfect" of its kind he had seen anywhere in the world, he declared that its ornamentation gave it a "lightness and elegance" which was "probably unrivalled".

The largest stele at Axum has long since fallen. Over 33 metres in length, and perhaps the biggest single piece of stone quarried in ancient times, it is engraved with decorative motifs similar to those on the standing obelisk, but with a design representing no fewer than 13 storeys.

Another interesting, but quite differently decorated stele, also now fallen, measures nine metres in height. It bears, on its front side, a column, carved in low relief, with a capital formed of two leaves supporting a mysterious object represented by a rectangle, surmounted by a triangle or pointed arch. These two latter emblems are also found, in a slightly squatter form, on the rear of the stele. The object they represent must, because of its exalted position, have been considered of great importance. What it was in fact supposed to be, however, is a matter of speculation. Some authorities have argued that it signifies a house or palace, others a grave, perhaps of an ancient Axumite monarch, while others hold that it is a representation of the Ark of the Covenant.

Taken as a group, the stelae of Axum are the most wondrous feature of this ancient and remarkable city. How, lacking modern technology and modern skills, did the architects and builders of the Axumite kings succeed in quarrying such massive monolithic blocks of solid granite from the surrounding hills, how did they transport objects weighing several hundred tonnes and how, finally, did they raise them up and embed them in the earth? There are no easy answers to such questions, and the visitor today will find his mind turning superstitiously to thoughts of magic, and of the mysterious intervention of the Gods in the affairs of men.

The techniques of cutting and transporting giant blocks of granite employed in the obelisks were also put to use in the construction of a large fortress on a hilltop which dominates the city to the north-east. Square in plan, this structure measures 27 metres on each side. The walls, which have long since crumbled, were projected at the corners to form four towers, which are thought to have had flat roofs crowned with

battlements. The entrance, divided by square pillars and three apertures, was reached by an imposing flight of stairs. Cosmas Indicopleustes, who visited Axum in the sixth century AD, reports that the "four towered palace of the King of Ethiopia" was adorned with "four brazen figures" of a unicorn, as well as the skin of a rhinoceros "stuffed with chaff". He also saw there several giraffes which had been caught "by command of the King when young and tamed to make a show for his amusement".

A number of underground galleries and chambers, roofed and walled with massive granite blocks fitted together with an almost supernatural precision, lie beneath the fortress. Local tradition identifies these catacombs as the tombs of Emperor Kaleb (514-542 AD) and of his son Gebre-Maskal. Each tomb is approached down a steep stone stairway, while at the entrance to the underground vaults a vestibule leads into three separate chambers with doorways carved to resemble those decorating the great stelae. Empty stone coffins lie within these deeply buried chambers which, according to one legend, once contained great riches in gold and pearls. Further rooms, as yet unexcavated, extend

Opposite: The ruins of an immense palace, said to be that of the legendary Queen of Sheba, still convey an idea of the impressive structure it once must have been. Over 50 chambers have so far been excavated and amongst the treasures unearthed are the remains of a drainage system, with granite gargoyles carved in the shape of fish, through which water once flowed; the floor of a large throne-room; and a well-preserved kitchen in which stand two brick ovens.

Overleaf: In the Park of the Stelae at Axum are located a number of pre-Christian obelisks, some of which are thought to be over 3,000 years old. The largest of the stelae still standing (left foreground of picture) is 23 metres high and is carved on three faces to represent a tower-house of nine storeys. Around the base is a stone platform, or altar, with bowl-shaped cavities and a border of vine leaves.

backwards from here, blocked off behind massive granite walls.

Returning to the centre of Axum from the tombs of Kaleb and Gebre-Maskal, the traveller follows a steep road that offers striking views over the old city to the park of the stelae and the churches of St Mary of Zion. It is an indication of just how much more remains to be discovered and excavated in Axum that the makers of the road unearthed beneath it, and around it on all sides, ruins of many other palaces and buildings, the remote origins of which are as yet unknown and unresearched. And at the foot of the road, to the left, stands a large deep water reservoir, the Mai Shum, which according to legend was once the Bath of the Queen of Sheba. Still in use today by local water carriers, a series of steps can be seen carved into its steep sides. Worn thin by the passage of time and by the tread of countless thousands of feet, did these steps once echo the words of the legendary Makeda as she came down to bathe, recounting to her followers the wisdom of Solomon? Only further painstaking research can answer this and other questions about Axum. In the meantime, the ancient city's atmosphere of mystery, of impenetrable secrets, remains a part of its charm — hinting at still greater mysteries, still deeper secrets yet to be revealed.

Invasions are an oft-repeated theme of Ethiopian history, with the coastal zone, because of its exposure, most frequently subject to attack and occupation. The country's geography, however, has always provided one formidable natural barrier to even the most persistent aggressor — the high, remote escarpment of the central uplands that begin its abrupt rise only a few kilometres inland from the Red Sea littoral. In times of trouble, Ethiopia's past rulers would withdraw deeper and deeper behind these mountain battlements, trapping and confusing their enemies in the maze of valleys and gorges that lie beyond.

One such retreat from fanatical Muslim invaders began in the seventh and eighth centuries AD, as the great Axumite Christian state began slowly to decline. Deprived of its outlet to the sea at Adulis, it stagnated culturally and was further troubled and weakened by the inroads of northern coastal nomads who had been won to the Arab cause. These troubles weakened the powers of the State and led — probably in the 10th century — to a revolt of the predominantly non-Semitic peoples in the interior, principal amongst them the Agaw, who had been brought under Axumite suzerainty many centuries earlier. A section of the Agaw had, however, already been converted to Christianity and it was among these elements that the later Axumite kings took refuge, shifting their capital considerably to the south of Axum which had become untenable with the loss of the northern and coastal provinces.

54

carried out, not by angels, but by Indians. It should be remembered, however, that the swastika motif, still seen in national dress, art and architecture, has a tradition in Ethiopia of 6,000 years.

Over the centuries innumerable foreign travellers have visited and been impressed by the Lalibela churches. The first visitor to describe them was the Portuguese priest Franciso Alvares who, writing in the early 16th century of the church of Golgotha, observed: "Its walls were worked in a fine fashion, also the windows and the doors with all the tracery that could be told, so that neither a jeweller in silver, nor a worker in wax, could do more work."

Later, having described all the other churches in succession, he concluded: "It wearied me to write more of these works, because it seemed to me that they will not believe me if I write more, and because as to what I have already written they will accuse me of untruth. Therefore I swear by God, in whose power I am, that all that is written is the truth, and there is much more than I have already written, and I have left it that they may not tax me with its being falsehood."

The churches at Lalibela have certain features in common, but at the same time differ widely from each other. They fall geographically into three groups. Six churches are situated in close proximity to each other north of a river called the Jordan which flows through the town in the rainy season, namely Beta Medhane Alem, or House of the Saviour of the World; Beta Maryam, or House of Mary; Beta Dengel, or House of the Virgin; Beta Qedus Mikael, or House of St Michael; Beta Golgotha, or House of Golgotha; and Beta Sellassie, or House of the Trinity. Another four stand to the south of the river, namely Beta Emanuel, or House of Emanuel; Beta Qedus Mercurios, or House of St Mercurios; Beta Abba Libanos, or House of Abba Libanos; and Beta Qedus Gabriel Rufael, or House of St Gabriel and St Raphael. One other church, Beta Ghiorgis, or House of St George, stands at some distance away to the south-west.

Medhane Alem, the largest of the churches at Lalibela, measuring 33.5 metres long, 23.5 metres wide and 11 metres high, is unusual in having an external colonnade on all four sides. These columns are oblong rather than square in plan and extend from the main plinth to the gabled roof, the projecting eaves of which they support. The seven columns at the east and west ends of the church are progressively lengthened towards the centre, for there is no pediment as in Greek temples.

On either slope of the gabled roof is a carved representation of an arcade of semicircular-topped arches. The edge of the roof is cut to form a broad perpendicular band above the column which serves as a cornice. The nave and aisles are supported by four rows of seven rectangular pillars, square in plan. They rise direct from the stone floor without

Right: Crowds, wrapped in shammas against the cold, gather in the grey dawn to await the start of a church service. Christianity is expressed in Lalibela in ways that provide a direct link with the ancient origins of the faith.

bases, and are surmounted by stone brackets extending from each of their four sides to support the continuous barrel vault of the nave and the lateral and transverse semi-circular arches of the aisles. The principal door is in the centre of the west front, but there are also doors on the north and south sides. The doors also have semi-circular arches supported by brackets. There are two rows of windows. The upper have round arches also supported by brackets; the lower windows are rectangular, and are filled with panels of pierced stone ornamented with a central cross. The courtyard of this church is the starting point of a trench which surrounds the entire complex.

Beta Maryam, alone among the Lalibela churches, has three exterior porches built out from the main structure. The building has a nave and two aisles formed by two rows of five rectangular piers. In the centre of the transept is a tall central pier which helps to support the barrel-vault of the nave. There are three chapels at the east end, each with its own alter. The capitals, which extend slightly beyond the top of the pier, are cubical but slightly concave, and are surmounted by four brackets, each

56

Below: In the courtyard of the church of St Mary is the 'Pool of Fertility', in which women who have difficulty bearing children are dipped on the eve of Christmas.

with an oval moulding surmounting one face. There is an upper storey over each aisle.

Above the west porch is a bas-relief of two equestrian figures, one of whom is St George engaged in mortal conflict with the dragon. In the interior the capitals and some of the arches and piers are beautifully carved and there is rich decoration of foliage, animals and birds, including the two-headed eagle. The frieze over the arcade dividing nave and aisles consists of alternate carved panels and windows which receive light from the exterior windows. This church has a much larger courtyard than the other churches. The latter contains in its walls two small sanctuaries.

The churches of Mikael and Golgotha, two of the most interesting of the northern complex, adjoin each other and are inter-connected. They are approached by a tunnel leading from the south of the courtyard of Beta Maryam.

Mikael has a nave and two aisles. The columns consist of clusters of four engaged rectangular piers, with capitals somewhat less in height

Opposite: An old priest, in the shadow of one of Lalibela's rock-hewn churches, reads the Scriptures to a young apprentice deacon kneeling at his side. Religious training often begins early in childhood.

Above: Under an awning Lalibela clergy leaning on prayer sticks celebrate the birth of Christ with drums and chanting.

than in width. These capitals are slightly concave at the outer corners, and are surmounted by brackets consisting of an oval moulding between two narrow fillets. These churches contain several interesting pieces of furniture, with fine ornamental carving, including a chair said to have been the throne of King Lalibela. A silver cross attributable to the monarch is also sometimes displayed.

Abba Libanos, one of the finest of the southern complex of churches, is unique in having been built, according to tradition, not by Lalibela, but in his memory by his widow Kebra Masqal. This building is also unusual in not being entirely freed from the mountain out of which it is carved. The interior columns support stone representations of lintel beams. There are only two arches, one at the west end, and the other giving access to the sanctuary at the east end.

Ghiorgis, or St George, is carved to represent a Greek cross and is loftier than the other churches, being 12 metres in height. On its flat roof, which can be inspected from the mountain above its deep courtyard, are two concentric crosses. The eastern arm of the church is occupied by a

domed sanctuary, while the western contains the main door. Subsidiary doors also face the west, so that all three are visible from that side. There are no disengaged columns. Two rectangular engaged piers rise direct from the stone floor without bases, and bear four arches which give access to each of the four branches of the church.

This fine structure stands on a lofty and elaborately contrived three-tier plinth. The lowest tier rises to the height of a tall man's shoulders, but the others are shallow. A flight of eight steps leads to the main door, the topmost step of which is extremely broad. The principal door has a shallow porch ornamented with mouldings. The lower window frames resemble those of the doors, but the upper ones have ogee arches and bracket capitals. They are more ornate than others at Lalibela. Some comprise three concentric ogee arches. Sometimes a loosely-coiled trefoil spiral substitutes the capital, and a couple of trefoil leaves interlaced with a cross top the arch. A string-course placed slightly above the porch of the main door is carried round the entire church. The others are found above and beneath the upper windows, and one in the wall-space

Opposite: At the entrance to his cave, a hermit of Lalibela sits quietly in the morning sun studying the Bible.

slightly above midway between the upper course and the roof. A fifth course is formed by a plain flat band which serves as a cornice edging the roof. There are similar courses in the interior walls. Chiselled in the walls of the courtyard are a number of roundish caves containing the tombs of deceased priests and monks.

The passing centuries have not been kind to the marvels that Lalibela carved. Subsidence and erosion have taken their toll, and some of the monoliths may crumble and fall before many decades are out if the necessary funds for restoration cannot be found. Nevertheless, the majority of the churches are still places of active worship, particularly during Ethiopian Christmas and Easter when many thousands of pilgrims converge on Lalibela from all parts of the surrounding countryside.

The whole town is, in a sense, a piece of living sculpture carved and dedicated to the glory of God. No one visiting here can fail to be stunned and awed by the remarkable human achievements that the churches represent. The techniques that went into their construction are lost

Opposite: The Lalibela churches are inter-connected one with another by a maze of tunnels through which the clergy and congregation pass. Historians speculate that these tunnels and alleyways must originally have been built for defensive purposes. Many have fallen into disuse and it is likely that the network of underground connections is far more extensive than the present-day inhabitants of Lalibela realise.

Left: A village perches on the edge of the deep rock-hewn trench that protects the northern complex of the churches of Lalibela. From their homes, which cling precariously to the lip of the chasm, the villagers have a stunning view over the roofs of the churches and the surrounding hills.

Above: Trekking with ponies or mules is the best way to explore the mountains of Ethiopia where steep climbs and high altitudes often make walking difficult.

forever to mankind in the mists of a remote and mysterious history where legend and fact intertwine on the edges of magic. But the churches stand still as monuments to the ineffable past, and to the power and the spirit of the ancient Christian faith — a faith that retains its hold in Lalibela and in the Ethiopian north with pristine and undiminished vigour. Just attend an early morning service in one of the rock-hewn churches to appreciate the accuracy of this observation: the heavy rhythmic music with an undertone of drums, the chant of the deacons, the congregation giving thanks or calling out for the mercy of God, the cool dark walls, the texture of the rough stone floor, the silhouettes of people standing, leaning on prayer sticks, or slumped down in obeisance — all these things constitute a tangible link with original Christianity. One can sense how commanding the call of this faith must have been and understand how, in distant times, it fired the imagination of millions and spread across the world. This was the church that performed miracles, healed the sick, raised the dead. The feeding of the 5,000, the story of Lazarus, and of Christ walking on the water, appear in this context

perfectly comprehensible. It is a context in which, to this day, miracles are believed to stem from the pure energy of faith focused through the lives of saints and holy men, and in which the testaments of the Bible stand as revealed truths that none may question.

More than 2,600 metres above sea-level, Lalibela enjoys a fresh and invigorating climate and a sky of the intensest blue that gives a lovely translucence to the high clear air. From the town it is possible to trek out in several directions into the surrounding hills on mule-back to explore the many other rock-hewn and cave churches of the region, or simply for the pleasure of a ride up steep winding pathways that afford dramatic and spectacular views of the Lasta range of mountains.

The joys of mule-trekking, and of Ethiopian mountain scenery, however, reach their ultimate perfection about 200 kilometres to the north and west of Lalibela in the Simien National Park, surely one of the most beautiful stretches of unspoilt mountain wilderness surviving in the world today. Here are several of Ethiopia's tallest peaks, including the towering Ras Deshen which, at 4,543 metres, is the fourth highest

Below: The Gelada baboon, one of Ethiopia's endemic mammals is the last surviving member of a group of monkeys once widespread in Africa. These animals have a complex social structure and live in groups of up to 400 individuals divided into 'harems' presided over by a dominant male.

Gelada are seldom found far from the cliffside — over which they plunge at the first alarm. Their browsing ranks are arranged so that the babies are nearest to the edge and males are farthest away. Strict vegetarians, who spend much of their time digging for the roots and bulbs on which they feed, the Geladas are also known as 'bleeding heart baboons' due to the red patch of skin on their chests. Another nickname is 'lion monkey' because of their splendid manes, which were much sought after in years gone by as head-dresses for highland warriors.

68

Below: The bizarre flora of the Simiens are giant relatives of plants found in the hedgerows and gardens of far-off lands in Europe, Asia and South America. The most spectacular of these is the giant lobelia, which grows slowly for about 15 years, then suddenly produces a flowering woody stalk about 10 metres high.

mountain in Africa. The principal camps, consisting of simple lodge accommodation, have been established on a line running horizontally across the national park. From any one of these — Lamalimu in the west, Sankaber, and Geech in the east — the traveller may venture out on foot or mule-back to discover the unique scenery, flora and fauna of the Simien range.

Sankaber, marking a rough centre-point, stands on the edge of a giant precipice and commands an astonishing view over a terrain which ancient seismic activity, followed by millennia of erosion, has left folded and fissured, cut through with steep valleys and dominated by isolated and jutting crags. Lammergeyer vultures wheel and turn effortlessly on the thermals between the looming cloud banks and the earth far below.

The lammergeyer, with its three-metre wing span and cruel, hooked beak, is a scavenger with an unusual technique. Indifferent to meat, it carries bones up to a great height and then drops them on one of the many rocky outcroppings of the Simien, swooping down to eat the scattered marrow. Other large birds found everywhere in these

Below: The Falasha village of Weleka at the foot of the Simien Mountains, where stylised figurines are sold in the pottery market.

mountains include the Thick-billed raven (indigenous to Ethiopia), the Ruppell's griffon vulture, the Egyptian vulture, and the Augur buzzard, the Wattled ibis (another indigenous bird), and the fierce Tawny eagle. With smaller insect- and seed-eaters like the Spot-breasted plover, the White-backed black tit, and the Black-headed siskin (all indigenous), the total bird population of the Simien is thought to exceed 50 species.

Wildlife is equally rich, with the Simien range providing the last remaining habitat in the world for the rare Walia ibex, a type of large wild goat weighing up to 120 kilogrammes, with long, curved densely-ridged horns. It is estimated that fewer than 1,000 individuals of this species remain in existence, although, fortunately for the trekker, one of their favourite grazing grounds is only a few hours' walk from Sankaber camp. Rarely found at altitudes below 2,400 metres, these lovely, shy creatures are hard to approach. Ecology has adapted them to live on nearly vertical cliff faces, where they can sometimes be seen in the morning or evening browsing on narrow, grassy ledges.

The Gelada baboon, which like the Walia, is another of Ethiopia's endemic mammals, is also found in the Simien (and, more rarely, in other mountainous areas of the country). Nicknamed the 'lion monkey' because of its characteristic mane of fine auburn hair, the Gelada is a polite and cautious creature quite unlike the more common baboons found elsewhere in Africa. The heart-shaped patch of bare, reddish skin seen on the chests of both male and female has given rise to another nickname for this species, 'bleeding-heart baboon'.

Geladas are strict vegetarians and are to be seen in large groups roaming over the grassy slopes of the high Simien, digging for the roots and bulbs on which they feed. Their social habits are generally cooperative and include much mutual grooming, which has the function of keeping the fur clean and free of parasites. At times, however, usually in competition for a female, fights break out between young males who give vent to sharp cries of warning and screeches of rage that are almost human in their cadence. Geladas, like the Walias whose habitat they share, are shy creatures and will run away if stalked, disappearing over cliff-edges onto the remote ridges and outcroppings below.

A third representative of Ethiopia's seven endemic mammals, the Simien red fox, or Abyssinian wolf, can also occasionally be seen in the national park, although curiously (given its name) it is far more common in the Bale Mountains far to the south and east. Neither a wolf nor a fox, it is in fact a member of the dog family, but the only one of its genus. It has a bright red coat with white undermarkings, and a black tail, and stands about 60 centimetres high at the shoulder.

The unique character of Simien wildlife is mirrored in the many unusual kinds of vegetation that make this region of Ethiopia a botanical wonderland. Close to the Equator, its great altitude accounts for the specialised ecology in which Afro-alpine flora can thrive. Here plants grow which are related distantly to species found in the tropical lowlands, but which have evolved in bizarre ways to cope with the climatic rigours of the highlands.

At the highest levels, above 4,000 metres on the upper slopes of Ras Deshen, the vegetation cover is reduced to mosses and lichen. Lower down, between 3,600 and 3,000 metres, there are extensive stands of giant heath, for all the world like vastly overgrown heather, intermingled with giant St John's wort — a knobbly, strangely formed tree that has smaller, and more mundane relatives in the hedgerows of Europe. Other 'giants' of the Simien include sphere thistles standing over three metres tall, and the giant lobelia which, in the last stages of its 15-year growth, produces long flowering stalks 10 metres high. We "may well wonder", asks one naturalist, "how a plant, most of whose relatives are found in South America, came to be established in the mountains of Africa. And why did it reach giant proportions? For the lobelias, like many of the plants of the African highlands, are more familiar as small herbaceous species a few centimetres high." Even the rose, rarely more than a bush in Europe, is found here as a huge tree with trunks which can often exceed 30 cm in diameter. *Rosa abyssinica*, the only wild rose native to Africa, produces a delicate soft-pink and yellow, five-petalled flower that adds its gentle magic to the ever-changing panorama of colour and light on the Ethiopian uplands.

Below 3,000 metres, around Sankaber camp the traveller first begins to encounter signs of human habitation — grassy meadows that provide grazing for sheep, goats and cattle, and terraced hillsides planted with cereals. The people of this region are Amharas, speaking the Semitic Amharic tongue which has been adopted as Ethiopia's official language. Farmers in a sometimes arid, often cold and none too fertile environment that suffers bitterly from erosion, they have a proud code of honour, of hospitality and of self-help which makes them a match for this high and remote homeland. Most are Christians, but there are also long-established Muslim communities here, as well as scattered settlements of Falashas who call themselves Bete Israel ('The House of Israel') and preserve traditions of an ancient migration to Ethiopia from the Holy Land, thus providing a living link with distant times.

Journeying south and west out of the Simiens from Sankaber, down a good gravel road to the town of Debarak and thence to the great and ancient city of Gondar, the traveller will meet Falasha people more and more frequently. Ethnically indistinct from the numerically dominant Amharas, and speaking the same language, they nevertheless have stayed true to their original Jewish faith — a cultural enigma that has led several visitors to proclaim them the 'lost tribe of Israel'. Just to the north of Gondar, after the long descent from the Simiens, the Falasha village of Weleka is well worth visiting for its pottery market, where attractive, but extremely fragile figurines may be purchased cheaply from eager vendors. The Star of David is a recurring motif and there are many representations of a couple lying in bed — Solomon and Sheba, no less! The Falashas today are numbered in their hundreds rather than their thousands and seem to be approaching the final stages of a long drawn-out process of assimilation into wider Ethiopian culture. In past centuries, however, Falasha kings and queens for a time enjoyed considerable power, although they stood aloof from the struggles between encroaching Muslims and the Ethiopian Christian state.

The slow retreat, south and westwards before successive waves of Islamic invasion, is one of the principal factors underlying the rise of Gondar in the heart of the highlands, as a capital of Ethiopian Christendom. As the decline of Axum was followed by the rise of Lalibela, so also was the decline of Lalibela's Zagwe dynasty followed, after several centuries of migratory royal camps, mainly based in Shoa, by the rise of a new state headquartered in the north-west of the country near Lake Tana and later settled in the city of Gondar, where huge medieval castles were erected as symbols of permanence and power.

The founder of Gondar was Emperor Fasiladas who, tiring of the pattern of migration that had characterised the lifestyle of so many of his forefathers, moved his capital here from Danqaz, 30 kilometres to the south-east, in AD 1636, the fourth year of his reign. Unable to rid himself immediately of the migratory habit, Fasiladas moved in and out of Gondar for several seasons but by the late 1640s had built a great castle here, which stands to this day in a grassy compound surrounded by other fortresses of later construction. With its huge towers and looming battlemented walls, it seems like a piece of medieval Europe transposed to Ethiopia, and evokes images of chivalrous knights in full armour on horseback, and of ceremonies full of pageantry and honour.

The exact date of construction of this remarkable edifice is unknown, however it was in existence by 1648 when it was inspected by a Yemeni Ambassador, Hasan ibn Ahmad al-Haymi, who described it as "one of the most marvellous of buildings, worthy of admiration, and the most beautiful of outstanding wonders". He adds that it was designed by an Indian "master-builder". In the vicinity of this palace there were, al-Haymi says, a number of other important buildings, albeit constructed of mud, which were finely furnished, containing numerous

Overleaf: The castle of Emperor Fasiladas at Gondar. With crenellated walls, arched doorways and domed turrets, it was the first of the six palaces to be constructed in this city which acted as the capital of Ethiopia for almost 200 years.

74

Byzantine beds or couches, with Indian mattresses, besides resplendent sofas embellished with ornaments and jewels, "unsurpassable in their beauty to the beholder".

The courtiers who occupied this part of the town were attired, the Yemeni notes, in splendid state, and were dressed in fine brocade adorned with gold braid and embroidered clothes of silk. The appearance of these exquisitely dressed nobles was so remarkable that anyone looking at them was "transfixed with amazement at the strangeness of the art". Around their waists they wore belts decorated with splendid and costly jewels which, al-Haymi declared, "belong to them in this world, but to us, God willing, in the next". These courtiers carried swords from Sennar decorated with the purest gold, and stood in lines according to their height; they wore gold rings and earrings which "flamed like fire and shimmered like pearls".

The castle of Fasiladas, which from the outset dominated Gondar, has been described by many foreign travellers. One of the first to do so was the Scottish explorer James Bruce who wrote of it in the late 18th century as a "structure of considerable consequence," a "square building, flanked with square towers," from the top of which one has "a magnificent view" of all the country southward to Lake Tana.

An even more graphic description was provided a century or so later by the British ethnographer and game-hunter P H G Powell-Cotton. Inspecting the much weathered edifice, by then a quarter of a millennium old, he observed: "The castle is two storeys in height, and almost square, the sides measuring 90 feet by 84; circular domed towers protect the corners . . . while at the south . . . the main building is carried up in a square, castellated tower, which dominates the rest to the height of two storeys, and against which the nearest circular tower rests, as though it were a huge buttress. The walls, which are six feet six inches thick, are embattled, the centre of the south-west front and the square tower each having a stone arch where a bell had been hung, from which the call to arms must often have been rung out. An inclined plane of masonry, little more than a yard wide, leads directly from the courtyard to the first floor, on which there are three principal rooms, the larger being 60 feet by 18, while the two others are each 42 feet by 18. These are lit by spacious openings, in many of which the double doors of solid Sankar wood still remain. The three on the south-east side opened on to a wooden balcony, which ran the whole width of the castle . . . The walls had cow-horns built in . . . as pegs on which hung swords and utensils of sorts. The staircase to the roof is in the square tower; opposite this, upon the platform, and close to the southern corner-tower, stands what appears to have been a small chapel with a vaulted roof. . . An outside stair, springing from the roof, reaches half-way up the large tower, the top of which was gained by a wooden stair, of which only fragments remain clinging to the wall. The roof and floors . . . are of concrete laid on beams."

In addition to this castle Fasiladas is said to have been responsible for the building of a number of other structures. Perhaps the oldest of these is the *Enqulal Gemb,* or Egg Castle, so named on account of its egg-shaped domed roof, which stands to the north-east of the main castle. Another edifice thought to have been put up at about the same time is a one-storeyed battlemented castle, further to the north-east, sometimes referred to as the *Kwali Gemb,* apparently because the ladies there decorated their eyes with *kwal,* or antimony, though others called it the *Duqet Gemb,* or Flour House, or the Building of Nuptials. Other buildings attributed to this reign included a small two-tower castle known as the *Wereqet Gemb,* or Building for *wereqet,* i.e. paper, which served as the royal archive and secretariat, and the *Beta Afras,* or House of Horses, i.e. the stable.

Beyond the confines of the city to the north-west by the Qaha River there is another fine building also sometimes associated with Fasiladas — a bathing palace which, according to others, may in fact have been built, or rebuilt, in the 18th century, during the reign of Emperor Iyasu II.

The building, as we now know it, is a two-storeyed battlemented structure situated within and on one side of a rectangular pool of water which was supplied by a canal from the nearby Qaha River. The compound is surrounded by a wall with an entrance tower and several smaller fortifications. The bathing pavilion itself stands on pier arches, and contains several rooms which are reached by a stone bridge, part of which could be raised for defence.

Another building possibly dating from this period was an isolated castle later used by Ras Mikael Sehul, a notable 18th-century ruler of Tigray and sometime master of Gondar. Other traditions, however, assert that this well-preserved structure was not in fact erected until shortly before Mikael's time.

Besides such secular buildings, Fasiladas is reputed to have erected no fewer than seven churches, as well as seven bridges which are still popularly referred to as *Fasil deldey,* or Fasiladas, bridges.

By the time of Fasiladas' death in 1667 Gondar was so well established that his son and successor, Emperor Yohannes I, made no attempt, like previous monarchs, to seek out a new capital for himself. On the contrary he spent even more of his time in Gondar than his father had done, and, though obliged to leave every year on expeditions, returned annually to spend the rainy season in the capital. Like his father he also erected a

Overleaf: Interior of the Debre Birhan Sellassie church at Gondar. Murals depict the Trinity, the Crucifixion of Christ, the story of St George and the dragon, and other religious legends. The famous painted ceiling is covered by faces of angels.

number of notable edifices, the most famous of which were a library and chancery, both about half the size of the original castle of Fasiladas, and standing to the north-west of it, besides several churches in or around the city.

The library, still standing today, is an almost square, two-storey battlemented structure with a terrace roof and walls finely decorated with crosses in red tuff. This building was doubtless a source of much pleasure to its founder who was described as "very pious and devout", a man of scholarly interests who "greatly loved books".

The chancery was a longer and somewhat larger building, also battlemented and of two storeys, with an imposing tower, and was ornamented inside with ivory. The edifice was erected, it is interesting to note, by an Ethiopian builder whose name has been preserved — it was the work, according to a contemporary chronicle, of a certain Wolde Ghiorgis who is said to have been "endowed with intelligence".

Yohannes was also responsible for accentuating the town's segregation into different religious quarters. The separation of Muslims and Falashas was decreed by Yohannes in 1668, after a church council held in the metropolis where the expulsion of the *Afreng*, or Franks, i.e. Roman Catholics, was also ordered. A large number of the latter accordingly left Gondar in the spring of 1669 when they were escorted westwards as far as the frontier of Sennar, and in the following year the monarch gave orders for the Muslims to move away from the Christians. This decree was probably not rigidly enforced, for it was repeated in 1678.

The status of Gondar was consolidated during the long reign of Yohannes' son and successor Emperor Iyasu, or Joshua, I (1682-1706), often referred to as Iyasu the Great. Like his father he made no attempt to establish a new capital, spent every rainy season in Gondar, and devoted much of his attention to the building of further palaces and churches. Some of his construction work was carried out by the Ethiopian architect Wolde Ghiorgis who is described by Iyasu's chronicle as "able, intelligent and of good renown".

The main castle of Iyasu the Great is second only in size to that of Fasiladas and stands next to it in the Gondar castle compound. It is an imposing battlemented structure with three towers, one with an inner and another with an outer staircase. Described by the chronicle as "finer than the house of Solomon", its walls were, in Iyasu's time, decorated with ivory, mirrors and paintings of palm trees, while its ceiling was covered with gold and precious stones.

Although it is much deteriorated today, a good description of this castle is provided by Powell-Cotton who, writing after all trace of decoration had disappeared, noted that the structure presented "several remarkable features", for: "The ceiling of the upper storey, instead of being flat, as in all the other buildings, is vaulted with brick ribs filled in with concrete; this storey is approached by an inclined plane of very shallow steps, which winds up the outside of a circular tower; a platform, now fallen, led from this tower to another at the north-west corner of the building, inside which a staircase gave access to the roof. The upper part is divided into two chief rooms, the larger of which is 33 feet long by 18 feet wide. In the walls are cavities, which I believed served as flues, heated by fires on the ground floor."

Another structure apparently erected during this reign was the *Feqr Gemb,* or Building of Love, said to have been allocated by Iyasu the Great to his father's paramours.

It was perhaps around this time that a *Makababya,* or encircling wall, was constructed around the principal castles, thus creating a clearly defined palace quarter.

Iyasu also arranged for the building of two fine churches. The first was that of Tekle Haymanot which was linked to the palace by a viaduct. It was in this church that the chronicles of Gondarine times were kept.

The other place of worship built by Iyasu was the church of Debre Birhan Sellassie, or Light of the Trinity, which still stands on raised land to the north-west of the city. This building has been described as a "stupendous and wondrous edifice". In its heyday it was surmounted by a gold cross with seven gold balls the size of ostrich eggs which are said to have shone like the sun by day and like the moon by night, while the inner walls were "marvellously" painted from top to bottom with innumerable scenes from religious history. The nearby belfry was equipped with two huge bronze bells, a gift from the Dutch Governor of Batavia, which when struck could be heard for miles around.

Gondar in Iyasu's day was the site of much ceremonial and pageantry which increased as the reign proceeded. Life at court was described by Charles Poncet, a French physician who visited the city at the close of the 17th century. Relating how he was "conducted thro' more than 20 apartments" he states that he "enter'd into a hall, where the Emperor was seated upon his throne. It was a sort of couch covered with a carpet of red damask flower'd with gold. There were round about great cushions wrought with gold. This throne, of which the feet were of messy silver, was plac'd at the bottom of a hall, in an alcove cover'd with a dome all shining with gold and azure. The Emperour was cloathed with a vest of silk, embroidered with gold and with very long sleeves. The scarf with which he was girt was embroidered after the same manner. He was bareheaded and his hair was braided very neatly. A great emerald glitter'd on his forehead and added majesty to him. He was alone in an alcove . . . seated upon his couch, with his legs across, after the manner of the Orientals. The great lords were on each side of him, standing in their ranks, having their hands cross'd one upon the other, and observing an awful silence."

On the following day, Poncet reports, "the Emperour was . . . clad with a vest of blue velvet flower'd with gold, which trail'd upon the ground. His head was cover'd with a muslin, strip'd gold, which fram'd a sort of crown after the manner of the ancients, and which left the middle beset with pearls. Two princes of the blood, richly clothed, waited for him at the palace gate with a magnificent canopy, under which the Emperour marched, with his trumpets, kettle-drums, flutes, hautboys and other instruments going before him, which made a good agreeable harmony. He was follow'd by the seven chief ministers of the empire, supporting each other under the arms and with their heads cover'd almost like the Emperour; having each a lance in his hand. He that walked in the middle carry'd the imperial crown, with his head uncover'd and seem'd to rest it, with some difficulty, against his breast. This crown, which is clos'd with a cross of precious stones at the top, is very magnificent. I marched in the same line with the ministers; habited after the Turkish manner and conducted by an officer who held me under the arm. The officers of the crown, supported in the same manner, followed, singing the praises of the Emperour and answering as it were in choires. Then came the musketeers, in their closebody's coats of different colours; and were follow'd by the archers, carrying their bows and arrows. Last of all, this procession was closed by the Emperour's led horses, richly harness'd and covered with costly stuffs of gold hanging down to the ground, over which were the skins [presumably of leopards or panthers], extremely beautiful.

"The Patriarch, in his pontifical habits wrought with crosses of gold, waited for him at the entrance of the chapel, accompany'd with near a hundred religious persons clad in white. They made a lane on both sides, and holding an iron cross in their hands; some within the chapel, and some without."

At the conclusion of this highly colourful ceremony, the Frenchman notes, "they discharg'd two pieces of cannon", after which Iyasu returned to the "great hall of his palace" where "he seated himself upon a throne rais'd very high; having on each side the ministers . . . All the assembly continued standing in a profound silence with their hands across. After the Emperour had taken some metheglin [i.e. mead] and some orange peel, which they presented him in a golden cup, those who had favours to beg came in and advanc'd up to the foot of the throne; where one of the ministers took their petitions and read them with a loud voice. Sometimes the Emperour took the pains to read them himself, and made answer to them out of hand."

Even more ecstatic accounts of the pageantry of Iyasu's day were penned by Ethiopian writers of the time. One described the monarch wearing apparel as "resplendent as the sun", while another claims that, though human, he "looked like a celestial angel".

The city by this time was a great commercial centre visited by traders from many lands. Poncet records that "All the merchants meet in a wide, spacious place to treat of their affairs. There they expose their merchandise to sale. The market lasts from morning to night. All sorts of commodities are sold there. Everyone has his proper place, where he exposes upon a mat what he has to sell."

After the death of Iyasu the Great in 1706, Gondar entered a period of political difficulty. Several subsequent rulers, among them the tyrannical early 18th century Emperor Bakaffa, nevertheless had further large buildings erected in the centre of the city. Bakaffa, according to his chronicle, constructed a fine palace which was decorated with pictures inside and outside, as well as, to the north of the palace compound, a long single-storeyed battlemented castle which is to this day associated with his name. Many more buildings were erected later in the century by his young son Emperor Iyasu II and widow, the redoubtable Empress Mentewab. The structures of this time were more elegant and far less rugged than those built by Fasiladas and his immediate successors.

One of the finest buildings put up in this period stands immediately north-east of Bakaffa's castle by the wall of the palace compound. Still referred to as Mentewab's palace it is a two-storey square castellated building leading on to an oblong structure, both with terraced roofs, supported by two towers, one square and the other domed, and decorated with large Ethiopian crosses of red tuff set in the stonework.

Iyasu, while still a young man, was also responsible for redecorating the old castle of Fasiladas and was helped in this, according to Bruce, by the arrival of a group of Greek artists from Asia Minor. Bruce, who may well have learnt of this from some of their compatriots still in the country at the time of his own visit in 1769, relates that, "a rebellion, massacre, or some other misfortune" having befallen the Christians of Smyrna, some of them made their way to Cairo where, "finding that city in a less peaceable state than the one they had left", they made their way to Jeddah with a view to travelling to India "but, missing the monsoon, and being destitute of money and necessaries, they crossed over the Red Sea for Masuah [Massawa] and came to Gondar. " These workmen included 12 silversmiths, "very excellent in that fine work called filligrane, who were all received very readily by the King, liberally furnished both with necessaries and luxuries, and employed in his palace as their own taste directed them."

With the help of these craftsmen and of "several Abyssinians whom they had taught, sons of Greek artists whose fathers were dead", Iyasu "finished his presence-chamber in a manner truly admirable. The skirting, which in our country" the Scotsman says "is generally of wood, was finished with ivory four feet from the ground. Over this were three rows of mirrors from Venice, all joined together, and fixed in frames of copper, or cornices gilt with gold. The roof, in gaiety and taste, corresponded perfectly with the magnificent finishing of the room; it was the work of the Falasha, and consisted of painted cane, split and disposed in Mosaic figures, which produces a gaier effect than it is possible to conceive. "The Emperor also began "another chamber of equal expense, consisting of plates of ivory, with stars of all colours stained in each plate at proper distances", though by the time of his death "little had been done on it but the alcove in which he sat".

Iyasu, Bruce explains, was so "charmed with this multiplicity of works and workmen" that he "gave himself to it entirely; he even wrought with his own hand, and rejoiced at seeing the facility with which, by the use of a compass and a few straight lines, he could produce the figure of a star equally exact with any of his Greeks".

Much pleased with the efforts and achievements of these workmen, he granted them many favours. "Bounty", Bruce says, "followed bounty. The best villages, and those near the town, were given in property to the Greeks that they might recreate themselves, but at a distance, always liable to his call, and with as little loss of time as possible."

He describes the Ethiopian metropolis as having a population of "about 10,000 families in time of peace" — which would suggest that the city had perhaps 60,000 or 70,000 inhabitants. They lived for the most part, he says, in houses made of clay, with thatched roofs. Most dwellings were surrounded by a "multitude" of trees, every house having "two or three planted round it, so that, when viewed first from the heights" the settlement appeared "exactly like a wood", especially during "the season of the rains" when it was "covered with a multitude of white flowers" and "appeared as covered with white linen, or with new-fallen snow".

Immediately to the south-west of the city, in somewhat lower land, lay the Muslim quarter where Bruce himself resided. He describes it as "a large town" of up to 3,000 houses "some of them spacious and good". Its inhabitants included a number of rich traders, the most important of whom was one Nagadras Muhammad, "the chief of the Moors at Gondar, and principal merchant in Abyssinia". Many of the inhabitants

Right: In an ancient setting, perched on the wall of the ceremonial bathing place of Emperor Fasiladas, a young Gondar minstrel strums the Krar *— a six-stringed musical instrument that has been played in Ethiopia since time immemorial. The Fasiladas Bath, empty for most of the year, is still filled with water every* Timket *when it is used for baptisms.*

were "employed in taking care of the King's and nobility's baggage and field-equipage, both when they take the field and when they return from it. They pitch and strike their tents with surprising facility and expedition; they load and conduct the mules into a body under proper officers, but are never suffered, nor do they choose, to fight on either side."

Gondar declined considerably after Bruce's time as a result of civil wars in the late 18th and early 19th centuries. The city nevertheless remained the most important settlement in the country, and as the political, commercial and religious capital of the realm contained its largest urban population.

Many 19th century foreign travellers came to Gondar, and not a few provide interesting glimpses of various aspects of the city's life. Most observers of this period agree that the settlement occupied a significantly smaller area than in the past for, as the Frenchmen Combes and Tamisier observe, "war, pillage and fire had greatly contracted its limits".

Yet, as the headquarters of the ruler, Gondar in the early 19th century was still, as the Frenchmen Ferret and Glinier observed, a place of fashion, the Paris of Ethiopia. They declare: "You often meet in the street Abyssinian gentlemen covered with clothes of dazzling whiteness. They are accompanied by numerous followers armed with swords, spears and shields. Their manners are noble and full of distinction. They have pretensions to politeness and good taste, love luxury, pleasures, the table and war, and like to relate exploits more or less true of which they have been the heroes."

The city's population included numerous soldiers and merchants, as well as lawyers pleading their cases, for the most part in the open air. The city's large market dealt in produce from all parts of Ethiopia. Gondar was also, at this time, the place of abode of the Abun, or head of the Ethiopian church, as well as of the *Echege*, or chief of the monks, both of whom had their official residences in the city, as well as of a large number of priests.

By the mid-19th century, however, the city lost its status as the capital of the empire when Emperor Tewodros, one of the founders of modern Ethiopia, transferred his Government to Debre Tabor and later to Magdala. The old metropolis suffered considerably during this period for, falling under the control of rebels, it was twice attacked by Tewodros, in 1864 and again in 1866, when the irate ruler destroyed many of its buildings, including churches, and carried off their treasures to his new capital. The decline of the city continued under Tewodros' successor Emperor Yohannes, or John, IV, who retained Debre Tabor as the seat of Government. Gondar, "widowed of its masters", both secular and religious, was thus reduced as the French traveller Achille Raffray noted, to a "gloomy and pining city".

The settlement suffered further serious blows as a result of war with the Sudanese Dervishes in the 1880s. The Ethiopian historian Blattengeta Heru Wolde Sellassie relates that the enemy, breaking into the city in 1888, "burnt all the churches. Those who were brave were slaughtered on the spot, while the cowardly fled. The remainder, women and children, were made prisoner and taken into slavery". Some months later the Dervishes again advanced on Gondar and "massacred the great and humble, the men and women whom they found". The extent of destruction in and around the city appalled the British traveller Powell-Cotton who, over a decade later, observed: "The nearer we approached Gondar the more numerous became the ruins of villages, farmsteads, and churches; the massive piles of ancient masonry, one could see by the jungle which grew over them, were relics of long-past days; but many ruins were of more recent date, being attributable to the raids of the Dervishes." Commerce, the Englishman explains, was likewise a mere shadow of its former glory. Recalling that the market was by then "a very poor one" and that he "could not get one half the supplies" he needed for his men, he declared, "Up to the Dervish invasion, Gondar, although no longer the capital of an empire, was still a considerable place, being, as it is, the natural centre to which traders converge from what is now the Italian colony of Erythrea, the salt-mines of Assal, the Soudan, and both shores of Lake Tana. Many rich Nagadis [i.e. traders] lived there, who despatched their caravans in every direction, but nearly all these lost, not only their wealth, but their lives as well . . . Now there is only one large merchant remaining in the place."

Gondar, by then full of ruins, was described by the German envoy Felix Rosen early in the 20th century as "a dead city which belongs only to the past". Most of the old palaces were in a tumbledown condition, and the majority of the finer private dwellings had been destroyed and had been superseded by small huts.

The return of peace after the war with the Dervishes led, however, to a resumption of trade. It was therefore not long before Gondar market began again to attract large numbers of buyers and sellers, and to handle a wide range of local goods. These included once more salt from the Afar lowlands, cattle, mules, goats and other livestock from Bagemder, honey and wax from the high Simien Mountains to the north, agricultural supplies of all kinds from lands south of the Blue Nile, ivory and gold from the Beni Shangul country in the west, civet from Enarya and Gudru, and coffee and cloth from Kaffa, as well as many locally produced handicrafts for which the city was still famous. These included jewellery of both gold and silver, besides articles of iron, horn and wood, pottery of all shapes and sizes, saddles and saddle cloth, church paraphernalia of all kinds, priests' vestments, and musical instruments.

Steps for the repair of churches destroyed by the Dervishes were taken shortly after World War I, and several of the palaces were later also partially or wholly restored. These developments coincided with the revival, throughout the 20th century, of the city's fortunes, and Gondar today is thus again a vigorous and attractive urban centre, and has a burgeoning population in excess of 65,000. The short period of Italian occupation in World War II saw the construction of many graceful villas decorated with balconies, vine trellises and shuttered windows, standing back from spacious treelined avenues in gardens filled with flowering shrubs. More recent constructions include the splendid 64-room Goha Hotel which commands a panoramic view southwards over the city and thence, across 64 kilometres of rolling, gently sloping farmland, to the town of Gorgora and the northern shores of Lake Tana.

Tana, Ethiopia's largest lake, occupies an area of more than 5,000

square kilometres in the watershed of the lofty mountains that surround it. For the traveller, the best point to begin an exploration of this beautiful inland sea is undoubtedly Bahar Dar, a relatively new settlement on the south-eastern shore which boasts several good hotels and a jetty from which motorboats and other craft can be hired.

Apart from its scenic beauty — which makes a visit to Bahar Dar and Tana worthwhile in itself — the lake has a fascinating history of its own associated with the Ethiopian Orthodox Church and with a tradition of monastic retreat. For hundreds of years men of religion have come here from all parts of Ethiopia to devote their lives to quiet contemplation amidst its calm serenity. On some 20 of the lake's 30 islands, ancient monasteries are to be found, some dating back to the 13th century and still inhabited today. Here small communities of monks isolate themselves from the world and its cares and dedicate themselves to meditation and prayer.

One such island, just half-an-hour's cruise from Bahar Dar by motor-launch, houses the 15th-century monastery of Kebran Gabriel. The island

itself juts out from the water like the tip of a submerged mountain planted over with rich green trees. Landfall can only be easily made at one point on the island and, from here, a well trodden path winds up under a canopy of branches. No women are allowed to set foot here, but male travellers may visit the island and the monastery without formality.

The monastery is situated at the very top of the island in a stone-walled compound. The church itself is a large circular structure in traditional Ethiopic design, with walls made of compacted mud and straw. It is an unassuming building that, nevertheless, has a cathedral

Below: Tankwas, *papyrus boats of ancient design, are the main form of transportation on Lake Tana and also serve an important commercial purpose as firewood carriers.*

Opposite: Monk of Ura-Kidanemeret stands in an open doorway leading to the Holy of Holies — the inner sanctum of all Ethiopian Orthodox churches which contains the Tabot (representation of the Ark of Covenant) and into which only the most senior priests are admitted.

atmosphere every bit as impressive in its own way as that evoked by the great European places of worship like Notre Dame or Westminster Abbey.

When not engaged in church ceremony, the monks of Kebran Gabriel work in the gardens of the monastery where they gain most of their sustenance. They, themselves, never leave the island, but the few young novices in training there do from time to time visit Bahar Dar to purchase necessary supplies.

Life at Kebran Gabriel is simple to an extreme, uncluttered and remote. Abba Haile Mariam who lived to over 90, was on the island for a quarter of a century and saw no reason ever to leave its shores. Draped in white and grey robes, he could be seen sitting on a stone in the garden and clutching a rosary of amber beads. He would explain: "Through isolation I get real happiness. All my days I have been loyal to God and will remain so until I die. I have cut myself off from the life of the world. I am free from its distractions."

Another monastery within one hour's cruising time of Bahar Dar is

Ura-Kidanemeret, situated on the Zegie peninsula. Because it is part of the mainland, its orientation is different from that of Kebran Gabriel. The emphasis on isolation is a good deal less and the monastery is clearly a part of the local community with children playing in its green and leafy compound and villagers coming and going freely. Women visitors are allowed and the monks are more open and communicative.

The church design at Ura-Kidanemeret is similar to that at Kebran Gabriel and, indeed, dates from the same period. It is a more decorative building, however, arched over with a huge conical thatched roof and superbly painted inside and out with colourful frescoes depicting scenes from Biblical lore and from the history of the Ethiopian Church.

Ura-Kidanemeret has a large treasury containing ancient, beautifully illuminated Bibles written in Ge'ez from which Ethiopia's modern Amharic language is derived. Many other texts and records are also stored here, bearing witness to the observation that the Orthodox Church through the ages has been one of the prime sources and repositories of written Ethiopian history.

Returning from the Zegie peninsula to Bahar Dar in the late afternoon across Lake Tana's placid waters makes a delightful and relaxing cruise. Cormorants follow the boat, swooping into its wake to dive for fish — of which the lake boasts many species including tilapia, white-fish, catfish and Nile perch. Villagers ply from shore to shore on low-floating papyrus canoes, called *tankwas*, loaded with firewood and agricultural produce. The design of these fragile craft is virtually as old as human settlement itself in these parts, and echoes ancient Egyptian boat construction. A single canoe costs less than two US dollars to make and is good for two months of work before it becomes waterlogged and has to be replaced.

A slight detour off the main channel between Zegie and Bahar Dar leads to a bay at the south-eastern end of the lake where the shore-line, demarcated by a rubble of time-worn basalt boulders and overgrown with the waving fronds of green papyrus reeds, parts unobtrusively to give exit to Ethiopia's mightiest river, the Blue Nile — here called the Great Abbay. A discernible current runs across Lake Tana from the mouth of another river, the Little Abbay, on the western shore. Because of this geographers now trace the source of the Blue Nile to the springs in which the Little Abbay is born.

Great rivers, like high mountains, occupy a special region of the human psyche. Of all rivers, however, only the Nile, flowing through Egypt to the Mediterranean Sea, can claim to have been the focus of man's imaginings since the earliest days of recorded history. From Greek and Roman times mystics and adventurers have speculated wildly as to its source. These speculations were given concrete expression in the expeditions launched by European explorers like Bruce, Speke and Burton in the 18th and 19th centuries. As a result of these expeditions we now know that the Nile has not one but two sources. The White Nile rises in Lake Victoria in Uganda, the Blue Nile rises in Ethiopia in the mountains to the west of Lake Tana. At Khartoum, the capital city of Sudan, the two rivers merge into one.

Of the two, the White Nile is by far the longest. The Blue Nile, however, descending 2,000 metres from Lake Tana to the plains of the Sudan, is the more dramatic and the more mysterious. To this day, stretches of the river in the wild and rugged highlands of Ethiopia remain inaccessible and unexplored. This is not true, however, of the source, which — long familiar to the people of the Lake Tana region — was first 'discovered' by Europeans in the early 17th century.

The earliest foreigner to visit the springs from which the Little Abbay rises, was a Spanish Jesuit, Pero Paes. Paes, a confidant of Emperor Susenyos, whom he soon afterwards converted to Catholicism, travelled with that monarch to the source of the Nile in April 1618. Describing his arrival in the area, which was known as Sakala, and recalling the interest which the origin of the river had evoked in previous ages, he reports that the water issued from "two springs round in shape, of which one might be four palms in diameter", and continues: "I cannot express what was my joy on seeing what Cyrus, what Cambyses, what Alexander, what Julius Caesar had so ardently and so faithfully desired to know."

A more detailed description of these springs was written at about the same time by another Jesuit, the Portuguese missionary Jeronimo, or Jerome, Lobo, whose account was later to be translated by the British lexicographer Dr Samuel Johnson. In this work, *A Voyage to Abyssinia*, Lobo recalls that the source of the Nile had been sought after in the past, at "much expense of labour", and had been the subject of innumerable "conjectures". Turning to the springs themselves he states that they consisted of two holes, each about two feet diameter, a stone's cast distant from each other. The one is but about five feet and a half in depth, at least we could not get our plummet farther, perhaps because it was stopped by roots, for the whole place is full of trees. Of the other, which is somewhat less, with a line of 10 feet we could find no bottom, and were assured by the inhabitants that none ever had been found. It is believed here that these springs are the vents of a great subterraneous lake; and they have the circumstance to favour their opinion, that the ground is always moist, and so soft that the water boils up under foot as one walks upon it: this is more visible after rains, for then the ground yields and sinks so much, that I believe it is chiefly supported by the roots of the trees that are interwoven one with the other."

The veracity of this account, and of Lobo's word in general, was fully accepted by Johnson who wrote in his preface that the Portuguese traveller appeared, "by his modest and disaffected narration, to have described things as he saw them; to have copied nature from life; and to have consulted his senses, not his imagination".

The Jesuit claim to have reached Sakala was, however, challenged a century and a half later by the Scottish explorer, James Bruce of Kinnaird, who had conceived the ambition of 'discovering' the source of the Nile himself, and was therefore reluctant to concede that any traveller had preceded him.

Bruce, who landed at the port of Massawa in 1769 and soon afterwards attached himself to the Ethiopian court at Gondar, encountered many difficulties, largely because the country was then in a state of civil war, but in 1771 achieved his goal of reaching the source of the Nile. Though a scholar and a man of science — he practised medicine extensively on his journey — he was not without his foibles, and refused, for reasons of vanity, to admit that the Jesuits had ever approached Sakala. In his five-volume memoirs, which bear the significant title *Travels to Discover the Source of the Nile* (Edinburgh, 1790) he declares that it was "easier to guess than describe the situation of my mind at that moment — standing in that spot which had baffled the genius, industry, and inquiry of both ancients and moderns, for the course of near 3,000 years".

Elaborating on this claim he observed, not without some pomposity, that kings had attempted the discovery of the source of the Nile "at the head of armies", but that each attempt was "distinguished from the last, only by the difference of the numbers which had perished". The result was that "disappointment" had "uniformly, and without exception, followed them all. Fame, riches and honour, had been held out for a series of ages to every individual of those myriads these princes commanded, without having produced one man capable of gratifying the curiosity of his sovereign, or wiping off this stain upon the enterprise and abilities of mankind, or adding this desideratum for the encouragement of geography." He, "though a mere private Briton", he proudly claims, had thus "triumphed" where "kings and their armies" had failed.

Such prose, however heroic, could not, however, blind the reader to the fact that its author's much vaunted 'discovery' had in fact been made by the Jesuits a century and a half earlier. Lobo's translator, Johnson, was one of the Scotsman's bitterest critics, and went so far as to observe that "when he first conversed with Mr Bruce, the Abyssinian traveller, he was very much inclined to believe he had been there, but that he had afterwards altered his opinion". Many others shared Johnson's view. The story is told that at a dinner party someone asked Bruce what musical instruments were used in Ethiopia. The author of *Travels to Discover the Source of the Nile,* not being prepared for the question, hesitated, and at last said, "I think I saw one lyre there." One of his fellow diners at once whispered to his neighbour "Yes, and there is one less since he left the country."

Bruce's egotism, and his refusal to concede that he was not the 'discoverer' but the 'rediscoverer' of the source of the Nile, should not prevent us from recognising his unquestionably real achievements, both as a traveller and as a scholar. His *Travels*, though incorrectly described as being "to Discover the Source of the Nile", is a work of major historical importance — a landmark in the story of Europe's discovery of Africa, and an invaluable source for our knowledge of 18th-century Ethiopian history.

For the modern visitor to Lake Tana the controversy as to who exactly first reached the Blue Nile's source must now seem somewhat esoteric and unnecessary. The Little Abbay springs have won their place in history, but there can be no doubt that it is not only the Little Abbay but also the whole of the vast water-system of Lake Tana that gives the Blue Nile the tremendous force and volume that carry it on a journey of more than 1,450 kilometres over giant cataracts, through deep gorges and, merged with the White Nile, across the parched and baking plains of Sudan and Egypt.

The power of the Blue Nile can perhaps best be appreciated just 30 kilometres downstream from the point where the river first leaves Lake Tana. Here a rumble of sound fills the air and the green fields and low hills on either bank seem to tremble with an echoed vibration. This vibration is the voice of the Blue Nile Falls, the most dramatic spectacle that either the White or Blue Niles have to offer and a vision of natural strength and grandeur unparalleled in Africa except for the Victoria Falls far to the south on the Zambezi.

Over 400 metres wide when in flood, and dropping over a sheer chasm more than 45 metres deep, the Blue Nile Falls throw up a continuous fine spray of water droplets which drench onlookers up to a kilometre away. This gentle deluge, in its turn, produces other phenomena — rainbows which shift and shimmer across the gorge with the changing arc of the sun, and a perennial rainforest of lush tropical vegetation. In the sky above, a Biblical pillar of cloud born of evaporation can be seen from afar, explaining the local name of the Falls — *Tissisat*, meaning 'water that smokes'.

The approach to the Falls on foot leads through Tissisat village, a market settlement of the Amhara people who live in this area farming crops like wheat, sorghum and *teff* (from which *injera*, the pancake-like national bread is made). Here the traveller will quickly find himself surrounded by a retinue of small, polite and insatiably curious children who see relatively few strangers and will walk all the way to the Falls with you, if they are allowed, for the pleasure of hearing your conversation. Dressed in simple woollen garments, carrying the sturdy walking sticks of the mountaineer, these self-appointed guides with their large, dark eyes and shy smiles make engaging and delightful companions. It is a tribute to the educational standards of rural Ethiopia that most of them speak English in addition to their own Amharic language. What a beautiful, serene and contented corner of the world this is in which to enjoy a morning's vigorous stroll and how little it hints at the astounding natural fury of the Falls set into it. After leaving Tissisat village the footpath to the Falls meanders first beside open and fertile fields, then drops into a deep basaltic rift that is spanned by an ancient fortified stone bridge built in the 17th century by Portuguese adventurers. A stiff climb follows, up a grassy hillside under the blue and breathless sky. Then, finally, the Falls come into view, breaking the smooth, majestic edge of the rolling Nile into a thundering cataract of white water foaming and boiling down a dark cliff.

Different people in different times visiting here have written with awe and wonder of the spectacle that the Blue Nile Falls present. Most, in one way or another have been mesmerised by the sight and come away in a mood of respectful contemplation: "The river," wrote James Bruce, who travelled to the Falls in 1770, "fell in one sheet of water, without any interval, above half an English mile in breadth, with a force and noise that was truly terrible and which stunned, and made me, for a time, perfectly dizzy. A thick fume, or haze, covered the Fall all round and hung over the course of the stream both above and below, marking its track, though the water was not seen. It was a magnificent sight that ages, added to the greatest length of human life, would not efface or eradicate from my memory; it struck me with a kind of stupor, and a total oblivion of where I was, and of every other sublunary concern."

The traveller to Ethiopia today can share the sensations that Bruce felt at the Falls, and witness the same endlessly recurring natural drama. The landscape has changed little — though modern Ethiopia has harnessed some of the tremendous strength of the waterflow to produce hydroelectricity. The people, also, are no doubt much the same — the hardy cycle of rural life on the high plateau around Lake Tana having

Overleaf: The Blue Nile Falls — known locally as Tisissat, *'water that smokes' — are amongst the most splendid sights in all Africa. Shimmering rainbows arch suddenly across the gorge, and the rain forest vegetation creates a restful contrast to the eggshell blue sky. Four hundred metres wide in flood, the smooth majestic edge of the rolling Nile breaks into a thundering cataract of white water foaming and boiling down a dark cliff.*

about it a timelessness and a permanence that mere passing years cannot erase. Here one has the sense of a settled, mature community which goes forward from day to day on the basis of clearly-defined and well-tried values. In the green fields and orderly villages, along the narrow, winding hillside paths, one finds plentiful evidence of a mode of human existence in near perfect harmony with nature.

Above all, however, the Blue Nile Falls are simply beautiful. An hour or a day spent before them is a rewarding and worthwhile experience no matter how cluttered or complicated one's life, or how rushed one's schedule. Such an experience is worth making time for and helps put more mundane concerns into perspective. Just sit for a while in the shade of a tree overlooking the Falls. At first the thunder of the water may overwhelm you; but, later, you will notice other things. High above in the endless spaces of the sky, eagles glide and swoop on the thermals. Below, in the gorge itself, smaller birds dart in and out of the spray — starlings with feathers of a vivid metallic blue, kingfishers, carmine bee-eaters, and tiny black-backed birds with brick-red wings that often venture onto perches in the cliff-face behind the Falls. The rainforest vegetation provides a lush and restful contrast of greens and lavender. Rainbows arch suddenly out of the water's depths, sometimes staying in place for an hour, sometimes vanishing or shifting position as quickly as they have come. It is impossible to visit a place like this without some subtle change being wrought in one's own outlook and attitudes — a greater consciousness of the wonder of creation, a more profound awareness of the loveliness and fragility of our little planet, a better and less arrogant understanding of man's place in the scheme of things.

Chapter Three · The City and the Wilderness

to return as the inquisitive are not well regarded at the palace . . ."

Menilek's victory over an invading Italian army in Adwa in northern Ethiopia on I March 1896, a decade after the founding of Addis Ababa, was followed by a considerable growth of the new capital. A number of Italian prisoners moreover were put to work in and around the city, especially in road-building.

To this period dates the erection of St George's church, the capital's second place of worship. It was a round building of traditional style, with a thatched roof, and not to be confused with the octagonal structure later erected on the same spot.

To the south of St George's, on slightly lower ground, lay the original Addis Ababa market, since relocated on a more westerly site. Occupying at the turn of the century a stretch of land measuring 1,000 metres long by 200 to 300 metres wide, it was attended each day by thousands of people, and on Saturdays by close on 50,000 purchasers and vendors. Powell-Cotton, who visited this market almost a century ago, observes that to it came "grains and spices, peppers and condiments from every corner of the kingdom, coffee from Harar and Lake Tana, cotton from the banks of the Blue Nile, gold from Beni Shangul, and civet from the Galla country, while salt from the far north of Tigray is the current change for the dollar. Fine cotton *shammas* [or togas], heavy burnouses of black, blanket-like cloth, jewellery and arms, saddlery and ploughs, all are here. In fact here you can feel the commercial pulse of Abyssinia, gain some insight into the present state of her civilisation, and gather what she has to offer in exchange".

Among the articles exposed for sale, then as now, were many curios, among them "thick silver rings, which are threaded on a blue string and worn round the neck, women's earrings in the form of highly ornamented solitaire studs, generally gilt, and curious earrings worn only by men who have killed an elephant, which are fashioned like elaborate finger-rings, sometimes with little chains pendent from them. There are also hair-pins with filigree heads, like those used for women's hats at home, tiny ear-picks in the form of spoons with variegated shapes and patterns, bracelets and rings, necklets of fine chain, and little charm-boxes as pendants, as well as crosses, plain or of filigree work". Describing other interesting sections of the market the same observer notes that: "Next to the raw-hide market, where you may usually find some leopard skins and occasionally a lion's pelt, are established the vendors of imported dressed and dyed leather, coloured to bright reds and greens for the decoration of saddles, bridles and cartridge-belts. There were also for sale the large, soft sleeping-skins which every Abyssinian loves to possess, and leather sacks for holding personal luggage while travelling by mule. In the crowded corner devoted to the sword-sellers you may see a petty chief, with one or two trusty followers, testing the blades of the big, straight swords taken from the Denishes, which may fetch as much as 10 to 15 dollars. Close by, other purchasers are examining the curve of an Abyssinian sword in its bright red scabbard, or perhaps choosing one from a pile of French blades made for the Ethiopian market . . . Nearby, at another stall, are exposed for sale circular convex shields of black buffalo hide, those for the populace ornamented by geometrical figures stamped on the leather, while those carried by officers are decorated with strips and bosses of silver, or of silver-gilt for higher ranks."

Although Addis Ababa's main market has been relocated and has subsequently grown and spread enormously in the decades since Powell-Cotton's visit, and although the range of its wares has greatly broadened, his description remains in many respects still accurate. No traveller to Addis Ababa should leave before taking a stroll through the Mercato which, with its vibrant colours, and the pungent aromas of incense and spices, makes a stunning impact on the senses.

Despite the presence of the palace, the churches and the market, Addis Ababa in Menilek's day was essentially a rural settlement, a character which, despite its modern expansion, it still retains to some extent in the 1990s, rambling over a vast area, with meadows and grazing grounds interspersed between high-rise buildings and modern Government offices. "What struck me most", wrote an English traveller, A E Pease, in 1899, "was the absence of anything in the nature of a town as we understand it, and the extraordinary way in which the population is scattered over the valley; single huts here, bunches of huts there, white tents pitched in groups." This picture is confirmed by Powell-Cotton who remarks that "dotted about the plain were clusters of huts, many stockaded enclosures — large and small — and several camps, but all very much scattered and more resembling a collection of villages and farmsteads than the capital of a great empire".

Movement within the settlement was moreover far from easy — particularly during the rainy season. "In the summer rains," observes Pease, "people are entirely cut off from one another, and at all times of the year communication is difficult, partly because the distances are long, and partly because the track winds up and down the water courses, so it takes a long time to move from place to place." Vivian, no less graphically, declares: "Streets there are none, and to go from one part of the town to the other you must simply bestride your mule and prepare to ride across country. Three-quarters of an hour at least are necessary for a pilgrimage from the British Agency to the palace, and as much again to

Opposite: The walls of Africa Hall, headquarters of the United Nations Economic Commission of Africa, are decorated with murals on glass by Ethiopian Master-Artist Afework Tekle. Also the site of the headquarters of the Organisation of African Unity is continent's premier diplomatic centre.

the market. On either of these journeys you must cross three or four deep ravines with stony, precipitous banks and a torrent-bed full of slippery boulders."

The difficulty of crossing torrents in the town was so great, Merab states, that a score of citizens were drowned each year in attempting to wade or swim across during the rainy season.

The extensive utilisation of timber in the construction of buildings and palisades, as well as the immense consumption of firewood for heating and cooking, and the absence of afforestation, soon led to an acute shortage of wood in Addis Ababa. "For two or three days before reaching the capital," wrote Vivian, "we had to do without wood in camp, for there was scarcely a tree to be seen. Every shrub that could possibly be used for firing had been cleared."

This dearth of wood was so great that late 19th-century foreign observers were convinced that Menilek would be obliged to abandon Addis Ababa, and that it would then fade into insignificance like Entoto before it. A B Wylde, a not unsympathetic British traveller who visited the capital in 1897, observed that the "immense straggling settlement" had "seen its best days", and that "some new place" would have to be chosen as the Emperor's headquarters, for it was by then "impossible to procure firewood for the wants of the inhabitants". Addis Ababa, he was convinced, was in fact "doomed". Count Gleichen, a British envoy, agreed, declaring "sooner or later a new spot must be chosen, for gradually all the wood is being cut down and consumed, and when the distance from the forest becomes inconveniently great, the capital must be removed elsewhere."

Menilek for his part was so concerned at the shortage of wood that he too contemplated moving the capital from Addis Ababa. In the autumn of 1900 he made his way 40 kilometres to the west where he started work on a new settlement which was later called Addis Alem, literally 'New World'.

The building of Addis Alem was carried out with remarkable speed. There are accounts of as many as 20,000 local peasants being mobilised for construction work. Pavilions, houses and an adarash, or reception hall, were put up, according to Lincoln De Castro, a doctor at the Italian legation, in "the briefest time", and work was soon in progress on a large rectangular palace building. The Viscount Bourg du Bozas' mission commented early in 1902 that Addis Alem was "the town of the future, as Addis Ababa was that of the present, and Entoto that of the past". The Italians were so impressed with this idea that, anxious to win Menilek's favour, and to regain prestige lost at the battle of Adwa less than half a decade earlier, they decided to move to the new town. They therefore began work there on a legation building which another French mission led by Jean Duchesne-Fournet described as one of the finest if not actually the finest in the country.

The proposed move of capital to Addis Alem was by then, however, encountering strong opposition, notably from persons who had already built costly structures in Addis Ababa, including not only the nobility, but also foreign legations. The British envoy, John Harrington, testily complained for example to the Foreign Office in March 1902 that, if the capital was transferred to the new settlement, "One will have to build another Agency there, with the possible result that as soon as the representatives have residences there the King will think the time has come for building another Addis something. The prospect of having to keep up two separate and distinct establishments and of flitting to and fro between them is not a very attractive one."

Opposition to the abandonment of Addis Ababa was also expressed by Empress Taytu who is said, by De Castro, to have declared that the palace at Addis Ababa was "the best" in the country and that there was therefore no need of any other.

Though Ethiopia had a long tradition of moving capitals there were by then strong reasons for not abandoning Addis Ababa, to which Menilek in due course bowed. A vast amount of resources had been invested in the existing capital. Work was moreover in progress on a railway which would link it to the port of Djibouti to the east, and any deviation of the line would be fraught with difficulties. Another factor of great importance was the advent of the quick-growing eucalyptus tree known in Amharic as *bahr-zaf*, or 'overseas tree', which was introduced from Australia. The first of these were probably planted by a Frenchman, Casimir Mondon-Vidailhet, who was followed by the Swiss craftsman Ilg and a French trader, Leon Cheeneux. The tree proved an immediate success: after five years it reached a height of over 12 metres, and by the time it was 12 years old it was 15 to 20 metres tall. Eucalyptus trees were soon being planted by the hectare, with the result that the capital which Wylde had described as "nearly tree-less" was within a decade or two referred to by Merab as a Eucalyptopolis, or Town of Eucalyptus Trees. These trees still contribute greatly to the charm and fragrance of the Ethiopian capital.

The coming of the eucalyptus trees played a major role in the future of Ethiopia, in that it solved Addis Ababa's then chronic shortage of wood, and thereby assured the permanency of the city. One of the inevitable corollaries of this, however, was that the plan to transfer the capital to Addis Alem was soon abandoned. Taytu, referring to the still incomplete palace building there, is said to have observed to her husband: "It is

Opposite: The streets of Addis Ababa rise and fall over a series of hills. In general, a person walking uphill may assume that he, or she, is travelling in a north-south direction.

better that this structure become a church in order that it may serve us as a guide to the Kingdom of Heaven." Acceding to her arguments Menilek rode in 1902 to the new settlement and, declaring that "the Kingdom of Heaven is worth more than the Kingdom on earth", gave orders that the building should be converted into a place of worship. It was accordingly dedicated to St Mary. The edifice was completed with the help of Menilek's Indian craftsmen who on one occasion, in 1904, staged a strike for better conditions — perhaps the first such event in Ethiopian history. This building, once conceived as a palace but now a church, stands today only an hour's drive from Addis Ababa, and is connected with the capital by a road which Menilek had built in 1902, the first such highway in the country.

Addis Ababa was the site, during Menilek's rule, of many innovations. Foreign travellers at the turn of the century were constantly commenting on signs of progress in the capital. Powell-Cotton for example describes the telegraph station as being built in the form of "a large circular *tucul*" or hut, "the roofs supported inside by a ring of posts, on which hung the rifles and shields of the guard". Though placed in this traditional setting, the office was well equipped, for the visitor could find "the latest invention in telegraphic and telephonic apparatus lying on tables of rough packing cases, side by side with a few *amole* (or bars of salt) and a pile of cartridge-cases (both empty and full), which have been received in payment for the messages sent". Powell-Cotton, another traveller of the period, reported seeing a rail which had been laid to transport building material to construction sites, but states that the people were too "conservative" to make use of it to any great extent. Menilek, he says, had also introduced wheelbarrows, but "the labourers only made use of them when they were under their master's eye. Directly they were left to their own devices, they hastened to their old accustomed method of carrying things on their backs."

Other innovations of the first years of the 20th century included a 2,400-metre race course, inaugurated in 1903; the first bank, the Bank of Abyssinia, founded in 1906; the first hotel, the Etege Hotel, in 1907; the first modern school, the Menilek School, in 1908; and the capital's first hospital, the Menilek Hospital, in 1910. A state printing press was established in 1911, and a hydroelectric installation on the nearby Akaki River some months later. Attempts were made also to set up a cinema, which met however with much popular disfavour, and was often spoken of as the *Seytan-bet*, or House of Satan.

The last years of Menilek's reign also witnessed a considerable amount of building, both public and private. One of the finest structures erected in this period was the new cathedral of St George, an octagonal building

designed by a Greek architect, Orphanides, and built by an Italian engineer, Castagna.

Many private dwellings were also put up, Dr Merab estimating in 1912 that there were by then almost 14,000 in the capital. The vast majority, however, were then still only mud huts, though about 200 stone houses were already in existence.

The capital's first brick factory was established in 1907, and four others, one owned by the Italian Castagna and three others by Greeks, were erected in the next few years.

Corrugated iron roofing began to be imported soon after the Djibouti railway reached Dire Dawa in 1902, and by 1905-6 no fewer than 50,000 sheets were purchased within a year.

Several well-made roads were in existence by 1903 when the American envoy, Robert Skinner, saw an "excellent macadamised" track leading to the British legation and wrote with enthusiasm of the "smooth and well-built roads" with which Menilek was "introducing modern civilisation." In the following year there arrived the first steamroller which was

Opposite and right: Addis Ababa children, dressed in brightly coloured robes, attend an early morning church service.

brought to Ethiopia by an Armenian, Sarkis Terzian, and was thereafter constantly at work.

The first two wooden bridges were erected, by French carpenters, at the end of the century, and the first stone one, by Russian engineers in 1902, after one of their number had been drowned swimming across a swollen river.

The growth of the city and the coming of many foreigners were also accompanied by significant changes in eating and drinking habits. Several corn mills and bakeries were in operation early in the century. Many butchers' shops sprang up a decade or so later — a notable innovation in that Ethiopians had traditionally slaughtered their own livestock. By 1913 the capital could boast two or three restaurants and as many cafes, mainly Greek-owned, as well as two hotels and no fewer than a hundred *tej*, or mead, drinking houses, which soon increased tenfold.

There were also significant changes in dress, largely due to the advent of the sewing machine. The American firm of Singer established a branch in Addis Ababa in 1909 and was soon selling hundreds of machines for 150 Maria Theresa dollars each, payable over many months.

These and many other developments in other fields symbolise the fact that Addis Ababa — which towards the end of Menilek's rule had a population of around 100,000, the largest market in the whole of Ethiopia, and covered an area equal to Paris within the fortifications — was the capital of a country with modernising aspirations.

An important event in the city's history was the completion in 1917 of the railway from Djibouti which greatly improved communications with the outside world. The years which followed also witnessed a steady increase in the number of motor cars — the first of which had arrived in Menilek's day; by 1928 there were no fewer than 500 vehicles in the capital. Traffic police were first appointed at about this time. The first airport likewise dates from this period.

A number of modern buildings were also erected, including several schools and hospitals and the railway station, completed in 1929, as well as the late Emperor's palace, now Addis Ababa University and the site of the Institute of Ethiopian Studies' fine Ethnological Museum, today a notable tourist attraction.

A solid mausoleum for Menilek and Taytu was built within the palace compound in 1930, and the Parliament building, now an important Government office, was constructed in 1934. Two cinemas and a well-frequented nightclub also came into existence in the period before the Second World War.

The Italian invasion in 1935, and subsequent five-year occupation, was a time of great hardship for the citizens of Addis Ababa, as for the people of Ethiopia in general.

Faced by the imminent occupation of the capital at the beginning of May 1936, a group of Ethiopian nationalists attempted to set fire to the city to prevent it falling into the hands of the enemy, as the Russians a century earlier had destroyed Moscow to deny it to Napoleon's army. Much of the commercial centre was destroyed.

On seizing the city the Italians immediately quartered in it a large occupation force. They were, however, initially reluctant to embark on building activity, for they envisaged transferring the capital to another site, on flatter, less elevated land. Construction was therefore limited to the erection of prefabricated buildings, mainly of wood. There was on the other hand a considerable amount of road-building, which was urgently needed, whatever capital was eventually chosen. After much discussion it was, however, decided to retain Addis Ababa, and indeed to make it the centre of government for a vast Italian empire embracing the entire Horn of Africa.

The occupation was vigorously opposed by Ethiopian patriots, some of whom worked secretly within the capital, while others operated freely in the nearby mountains, as well as throughout much of the rest of the country. Patriot forces launched two attacks on the city, in the summer of 1936, but were unable to capture it. Their resistance led to many reprisals including the execution in public of an Ethiopian bishop, Abuna Petros, or Peter, a statue of whom was later to be erected on the site. An attempt on the life of the fascist Viceroy, Graziani, by two Ethiopians from Eritrea, Abraha Debotch and Mogos Asgedom, in February 1937 provoked the Italians to unleash a three-day reign of terror in the course of which thousands of innocent Ethiopian citizens were killed in cold blood, and many of their houses were burnt down. Undeterred by the massacre and many other acts of repression, the Ethiopian resistance refused to abandon the struggle which continued throughout the entire period of fascist rule.

Having decided on the retention of Addis Ababa as the capital, the Italians began a grandiose building programme, conceived, as they proclaimed in racist terms, with a view to creating a metropolis with an anticipated European population of 200,000. Italians were to be settled to the east and the south of the city, while Ethiopians were to be relegated to the west. Two residential quarters were constructed for the exclusive use of Italians: one, for officials, was built by a parastatal organisation, the Istituto Nazionale per le Case degli Impiegati cello State, on which account the area is to this day known as Casa I N C I S; the other, for Italian workers, is spoken of as Casa Popolari. Ethiopians occupying

houses in the area designated for Europeans were evicted and moved to
the west of the city. The market, which had been situated below St
George's cathedral since Menilek's day, was likewise shifted westwards,
to its present site, an area sometimes referred to as 'Addis Ketema', or
'New Town', but most frequently known simply as the 'Mercato'. Indian
merchants, who until then had been prominent in the city's trade, were
criticised for their British connections and for the most part expelled.

The occupation also witnessed the erection of a number of imposing
buildings of concrete, mainly for governmental or parastatal use, as well
as the establishment of a temporary airport, with wooden structures, and
the digging of two water reservoirs outside the city, at Gafarsa and Abba
Samuel, to the west and east respectively. Much use was, however, also
made of pre-war buildings, among them schools and hospitals, which
were again put into service, but now mainly for Italians rather than
Ethiopians. It was symptomatic of the times that at the moment of the
fascist collapse in 1940 most Italian structures were no more than
blueprints, and that the Governor had his office in the former Emperor's
palace.

Mussolini's entry into the European war, in June 1940, led Britain to
decide on the destruction of Italian power in East Africa. Fascist rule in
Addis Ababa came to an end in April 1941, after which the city's large
temporary Italian population was repatriated, the colour bar was lifted
and the old Ethiopian Government was restored. Several streets were
renamed in honour of Allied leaders and wartime commanders.

The years which followed saw the establishment, or re-establishment,
in the city of various ministries and Government institutions, as well as
of a number of foreign companies and, later, offices of international
organisations.

The capital's architecture began to change in the late 1950s and early
1960s which witnessed the construction of a number of much larger and
more modern buildings than previously seen. The first of these was the
new Arts building of Addis Ababa University College, now part of
Addis Ababa University's Faculty of Science, a five-storey building, with
continuous bands of windows, designed by a British architect, C A
Fallek. This fine structure, which created considerable excitement when it
was first erected, was soon outclassed by many larger buildings, among
them Africa Hall, headquarters of the UN's Economic Commission for
Africa, designed by two Italian architects from Eritrea, Fenano and
Mezzedimi, and, in a particularly imposing position, the Addis Ababa
City Hall. Other buildings of interest include the Jubilee Palace, now
called the National Palace and used for various state occasions, and the
Hilton Hotel which has a large swimming pool fed with water from a

thermal spring. Addis Ababa's present-day appearance owes much to the fact that the city evolved rapidly out of a military camp and is situated on the slopes of the Entoto mountains.

The visitor seeking orientation in the now extensive Ethiopian metropolis should realise that it sprawls over a wide stretch of land descending from the Entoto heights in the north to much lower, and flatter, country to the south. A complication is, however, introduced by the fact that the slopes of Entoto are trisected by streams or torrent beds. These valleys are important in that they divide the city into three main sections.

To the east lies what may be termed the governmental and educational sector where one finds, roughly from north to south, the University, in several distinct campuses), the principal containing the fine Institute of Ethiopian Studies ethnographic museum; the National Museum with its notable historical and archaeological holdings; the Menilek School, the country's earliest establishment of modern education; the first state printing press; the Ministry of Education; the Sellasie cathedral (where many of the patriots of the 1936-41 war are buried); the old Menilek palace (still used for Government business) with the adjacent Menilek Mausoleum; the Mapping and Geography Institute, where numerous maps of the country may be obtained; the Ministry of Foreign Affairs (with the Hilton Hotel opposite); the Jubilee Palace, now the National Palace; the Filwoha Thermal Baths — well worth a visit; the Ghion Hotel; and Revolution Square with the office of the Ethiopian Tourism Commission facing it.

The central sector, which is devoted largely to commerce but in part also to Government business, runs from St George's cathedral and the City Hall and television studio in the north, by way of Churchill Road (the site of several shops catering for the tourist), to the railway station in the south. This sector houses the headquarters of the National and Commercial Banks; the main sales office of Ethiopian Airlines; the Post, Telephone and Telegraph Office; as well as the principal hospital, called Tikur Anbassa (the Black Lion); the National Theatre; several cinemas, the football stadium and two shopping centres, one on a road going eastwards to the University, and the other in the south, between the Airlines' office and the railway station.

The western sector, which is also much involved in trade, albeit less 'Westernised', is the site of the Mercato the city's main market, and also the location of the principal mosque and of many shops less frequented by foreign visitors. The south-western sector of the city, which developed later than the centre, is partially residential and partly industrial. It also houses an interesting art museum in which paintings by modern

Ethiopia's premier artist, Afework Tekle, are often displayed.

The fact that the metropolis developed out of a military camp has had several significant consequences. One is that the city is essentially scattered, for different quarters of the town grew up initially around the separate camps of Emperor Menilek and his various lords. Another result is that the houses of the rich, constructed perhaps for those lords or their heirs, and those of the poor, some of them maybe the descendants of the noble's servants and camp followers, are often situated in close proximity to each other, though zones of different types of housing have of course also come into existence, particularly in more recent years. Several of the older embassies, dating back to Menilek's day, including the Italian, British, French, Russian and German, lie on the north-eastern periphery of the city while those of countries more recently accredited to Ethiopia, including some of the recently independent African states, stand on other roads, including those to the new and old airports, to the south-east and south-west respectively.

Addis Ababa today is a fascinating city to visit. It boasts several excellent hotels and has a delightfully invigorating highland climate. From here, at the geographical centre of this vast country of more than a million square kilometres, roads branch out in all directions to the provinces beyond. One of these roads, running almost due west, passes the aborted royal camp of Addis Alem, the 'New World' that would, perhaps, have been the capital of Ethiopia today had Emperor Menilek not discovered the fast-growing virtues of the eucalyptus tree. A fitting symbol of the glory that Addis Alem aspired to but never quite achieved, the eucalyptus groves that supply Addis Ababa with its firewood extend this far and beyond, filling the air with a gentle fragrance and diffusing a soft green light on many stretches of the road.

Past Addis Alem, the next main settlement through which the western highway runs is Ambo, which is also known poetically as Hagare Hiwot — 'Land of Life'. Here there is a first-class hotel, and one of the many restorative hot-springs for which Ethiopia is famous has been harnessed to fill a swimming pool surrounded by lawns and shady trees. The sparkling mineral water 'Ambo' that graces most tables in Ethiopia is bottled in this town which is rapidly growing into an important industrial area.

Westwards again, beyond Ambo, the traveller enters the country's premier wine-growing district centred on the town of Guder, after which a popular export-quality red wine has been named. Vineyards stretch out across the rolling dun-coloured slopes on both sides of the road, interspersed with picturesque farmhouses and villas constructed from rough-hewn sandstone and with red-tiled roofs. Here, in the western reaches of Shoa, the landscape has a Mediterranean character reminiscent of the mimosa-clad hills of Provence or northern Italy.

The border between Shoa and its western neighbour Wollega is crossed at the village of Bako where vineyards give way to extensive coffee plantations tended by industrious farmers of Oromo stock, who make up the bulk of the population in this region. The principal town of Wollega is Nekemte, a substantial marketing and coffee-forwarding centre about 320 kilometres west of Addis Ababa. For all its economic importance, Nekemte is somewhat drab and undistinguished and for this reason the majority of travellers pass quickly through it, turning south on the Bedele road that leads out of Wollega into Illubabor which, with its tropical rainforests and abundant wildlife is surely Ethiopia's most exotic region.

As if to mark the ecological and environmental transition between Wollega and Illubabor, the highway enters a long sloping valley soon after Nekemte and crosses the tree-lined course of the Dedessa River before rising again towards Bedele through lush green rolling farmland heavily planted with coffee and sorghum.

After Bedele the road turns westwards again, forcing its way through countryside that becomes increasingly forested and overgrown and that, despite its rich soils, has only been marginally cleared for farming. Thatched circular homesteads rise out of small banana plantations and vegetable gardens, but seem threatened at any time to be overrun by the encroaching jungle. The traveller who has visited tropical West Africa or the more densely-wooded part of South-East Asia will find reminders of these untamed forest environments here. Colobus monkeys with distinctive black and white coats and clever wizened faces chatter in the leafy branches that overhang the road and move in troops across such fields as there are, uprooting seedlings in search of food and remorselessly undoing the work of the local farmers. After a journey through the highlands of northern Ethiopia which have been tamed to the plough for millennia, it comes as a startling surprise, here in the west, less than 500 kilometres from Addis Ababa, to find mankind once again in direct competition with the forces of the wilderness — a competition that is none too easily won.

The first main town of Illubabor is Metu, surrounded by singing forests filled with brightly plumed birds. The mood here is that of a frontier settlement, the frontier being not a political one but rather the intangible borderline between raw nature and the endeavours of man. Ethiopia's Oromo people, who have committed themselves to pushing this frontier back in their steady westwards expansion, crowd into Metu on holidays and weekends, drinking and listening to music in its many

Below: In Illubabor province, near
the village of Bechu, the Sor
waterfall pours into a lushly
overgrown natural amphitheatre.

small bars, or offering their produce for sale in its open market — produce that includes berries and wild honey as well as the more familiar grains and vegetables of established agriculture. At night a small generator chugs and puffs bravely for an hour or two before it is closed down, and then darkness and silence together fall over the town like a veil through which, at impossible distances, the bright stars blink and sparkle in the wheeling vault of the sky.

A 13-kilometre detour off the main western road out of Metu leads the traveller to the village of Bechu, which occupies an irregular clearing in the midst of a dense thicket of trees. From here, an hour's downhill walk through green glades on a narrow and at times barely discernible path, is rewarded with a view of one of Ethiopia's many splendid waterfalls where the Sor River pours over the lip of a broad sheer chasm 100 metres deep. A natural amphitheatre, heavily overgrown with weird cacti and tall grasses, this is a delightful spot in which to savour the primal atmosphere of Illubabor and to catch a glimpse of nature as it must once have been throughout much of Africa before the coming of man.

The province has other surprises yet, however. Just past the town of Gore, the regional capital 612 kilometres from Addis Ababa, the massive central escarpment that is Ethiopia's most notable geological feature quite suddenly comes to an end, dropping abruptly away towards the red and barren plains of the Sudan. Here the highland peoples, ever reluctant to venture down into the burning deserts that surround them on all sides, have their westernmost settlement. Dressed in warm clothing and goatskin caps to fend off the chill of the evening air at 2,000 metres, they have established a colourful market on the very edge of the escarpment to which the plain-dwellers sometimes venture up with their trade, strangers in a strange land, speaking languages that are totally unrelated to the Amharic and Oromo tongues that dominate much of the rest of Ethiopia.

Past Gore market the road enters a series of expansive winding curves that take it a thousand metres down to a broad plateau covered in scrub vegetation, acacia trees and dense brush. From here in a second giant step, carried through hairpin bends that overlook slopes of landslide-prone shale, the road descends the final stubborn foothills of the escarpment — withered and eroded rocks cut through with steep gullies. Sparsely wooded, these ancient hills are subject to bush fires that have denuded them even more of their thin vegetation cover, exposing the fragile topsoil to flash-floods and the unmerciful attentions of wind, rain and sun. In this uncongenial environment no agriculture is possible, and even the wild creatures, so common elsewhere in Illubabor, do not choose to live here. A few lonely Colobus monkeys perch forlornly on

124

the blackened branches of scorched and dying trees but otherwise only lizards and snakes, rustling drily, are truly at home amongst the naked rocks.

At the foot of the escarpment, funnelled through narrow walls of forbidding basalt, a permanent watercourse marks yet another profound ecological change. Here the Baro, the greatest river of Illubabor, ends its dramatic plunge from the mountains and embarks on a lazy meandering course across the western Ethiopian lowlands to the border of the Sudan, eventually emptying itself into the broad body of the White Nile above Khartoum. It is after crossing the Baro that the traveller first begins to encounter in any numbers the Nilotic peoples of Ethiopia, the Anuak and the Nuer, whose curious round houses with low doorways and many-tiered thatched roofs dot the sandy plains below. Long-limbed and dark-skinned, they are often scantily clad or wear nothing at all — a very sensible response to the extreme heat and humidity of this tropical lowland zone. Groups of women, bent forward under the weight of huge round calabashes filled with water, tall men armed with fierce spears

Above: Shoe-cleaner in Gore market enjoys a moment of good-natured fun with a younger-than-usual client.

Left: A man of Gore wearing a goatskin cap typical of the highland areas of Illubabor.

following their longhorn cattle, droves of cheerful inquisitive children running out from the villages, ostriches and scattered herds of plains game are amongst the sights that greet the traveller as he continues his journey west.

Through these simple and unsophisticated surroundings the road follows the widening course of the Baro, finally crossing it again at Gambela on an elegant and modern single span bridge — the longest of its kind in Ethiopia. The view from the bridge over this riverside town presents an exotic spectacle of soft orange flamboyants and mauve jacaranda trees amidst elegant villas set back from wide and leafy streets. In the waters below, children fish and townspeople come down to bathe — apparently indifferent to the numerous small crocodiles that sun themselves upon the sandspits.

Gambela has the charming, somewhat run down, slightly passé atmosphere of a once great tropical town. And this is exactly what it is, for at the turn of the century it was a major river port that, through the Sudan, acted as an outlet for a substantial share of Ethiopia's rich coffee trade. The establishment of a commercial station on the Baro was first envisaged at the end of the 19th century, as a step towards the formation of an inland shipping service linking that river with Khartoum, and more generally Ethiopia with the Sudan and Egypt. This move seemed of mutual advantage to both the British and Ethiopian Governments of the time. For Britain, which was then in control of the Sudan, the proposed service offered an opportunity of opening up trade with western, and conceivably also central, Ethiopia which, on account of the railway connecting Addis Ababa with Djibouti, might otherwise have been entirely dependent on France. The scheme was the more attractive in that the riches of Ethiopia were thought to be found primarily in the west of the country. This project was also advantageous to Emperor Menilek, who saw it as affording an opportunity of developing the commerce of a hitherto isolated area, as well as a way of asserting his independence of the French colonial Government in Djibouti with which he was then at loggerheads.

To further these objectives it was decided that Menilek should grant the British an enclave on the Baro River. This was effected by an agreement signed by the Emperor and the British representative in Addis Ababa, Captain Harrington, in May 1902. It stated that Ethiopia granted the British Government of the Sudan an area at Itang on the Baro River not exceeding 400 hectares "to be administered and occupied as a commercial station" so long as the Sudan remained under Anglo-Egyptian rule.

Subsequent study revealed that Itang was unhealthy and that a site further upstream would permit river communication for a longer part of the year. An alternative location was therefore chosen. It became known as Gambela, and was inaugurated as an internal port and customs post in 1907.

Steamers, which took seven days to sail down from Gambela to Khartoum, and 11 days to return against the current, were soon plying between the two places. Vessels sailed twice a month throughout the rainy season, usually from 21 June to 4 October. During the remainder of the year there was no service as there was insufficient water to allow shipping.

Gambela soon grew into a major trading centre. It handled the export from Ethiopia of coffee, wax and, to a lesser extent, skins, and the import of cotton cloth, salt and sacks, as well as various provisions and liquors.

The town, which prospered on this lucrative trade, differed from most Ethiopian settlements in that it was built according to a plan. It therefore had straight roads and strictly aligned buildings. These included the residence and office of the local British Commissioner, for many years

Captain J K Maurice, besides a sub-office of the Bank of Abyssinia, later the Bank of Ethiopia, and the dwellings of many foreign merchants, mainly Greeks. Beyond the compound there was an Ethiopian settlement clustered around the customs post and telegraph station, and the premises and warehouses of the Ethiopian Motor Transport Company.

The enclave reverted to Ethiopian rule after the independence of the Sudan, and the shipping service to Khartoum that had operated for almost half a century ceased in 1955. Gambela today, however, retains many echoes of its past glory. The warehouses still remain, although they are now only used to service local trade to points along the Baro River system inside Ethiopia. The old wharves, solidly built, have been hardly touched by the passing years and, standing on them, looking out over the wide curve of the river, it is not difficult to imagine the great steamers and flotillas of small vessels that once gathered here. The Ethiopian Government has plans in hand to reactivate and redevelop the facilities at Gambela and it is to be hoped that the river trade can be resumed, returning to this region much of its lost economic importance. In the meantime, this sleepy town with its lazy, relaxed lifestyle dominated by the long noontime siesta, holds many attractions for the traveller, providing a convenient gateway to the broad vistas of the western Ethiopian plains.

A rough track, often flooded in the rainy season, follows the northern bank of the Baro as it flows out of Gambela towards the Sudanese border, some 130 kilometres distant. The terrain is flat, marshy in places, and generally fertile; however there is little tradition of agriculture. The indigenous Anuak people are mainly fisherfolk in this region, and such crops as they do grow — mostly sorghum, used to produce a sour-flavoured porridge and an intoxicating country beer — do not reach their full potential because of the extremely primitive methods of cultivation employed. Birds and wild pigs are a constant nuisance in the planting season, and the numerous odd basket-like structures, open at both ends and mounted on platforms, that the traveller sees when passing through this terrain are in fact shelters for children whom the Anuak send out into the fields during planting to scare scavengers away.

There are few large villages, people preferring instead to group together around a mango grove in an extended family compound of no more than five or six huts. These buildings, used purely as sleeping quarters, have floors of polished, compacted mud, extremely low doorways let into walls decorated with engraved patterns depicting animals and magical symbols, and straw roofs that often extend down almost to ground level. During daylight hours the majority of family members stay in the open air, fishing, attending to the chores in the fields

Below: The townspeople of Gambela make use of the gently-flowing waters of the Baro River for a pleasant afternoon dip. With bright flamboyant trees and gracious avenues, Gambela has an atmosphere of past prosperity.

Overleaf: Vision of rural tranquillity: two Nuer boys playing 'catch' silhouetted against splendid purple of the night sky in western Ethiopia.

or simply lounging in the shade of the leafy mango trees and smoking long pipes of heady aromatic tobacco. The women, naked to the waist, wear elaborate bead necklaces and heavy ivory and bone bangles above the elbow, and have their hair closely cropped and sometimes their heads shaven. Both men and women indulge a further decorative fancy common amongst all the Nilotic peoples of Ethiopia and the Sudan, of having the front six teeth of the lower jaw removed at about the age of twelve.

As the track meanders along the course of the Baro further and further to the west of Gambela, the town's modernising influence fades and the traveller finds himself among people who have rarely, if ever, seen foreigners and whose contacts with the influences of the industrial era are remote in the extreme. Only since the late 1970s have Government-established schools begun to reach the children of this area and, for the majority of the population, the 20th century still remains just a distant rumour. Here the pace of human life can have changed little since the Stone Age, yet it has about it a decency, simplicity and gentle non-

acquisitive charm that surely should not be tampered with too harshly.

The Baro, at this point, is a poignantly beautiful river, rich in birdlife — geese, egrets, ibises, kingfishers and pelicans — and decorated with the greens and purples of floating water-hyacinth. Fish stocks are plentiful, both in the river itself and in the pools and lakes that flooding creates in the near reaches of the surrounding countryside. Everywhere long-legged men and children can be seen, waist-deep in water, stabbing for catfish amongst the reeds or casting string lines baited with simple lures from the low banks.

Past Itang, a sizeable settlement, the Anuak give way to their cousins the Nuer, who, though they also fish, are primarily cattle herders. Nuer are more social in their habits than the Anuak and live together in villages of several hundred souls at widely separated intervals along the river banks. They are a comely people, with long handsome faces and extremely dark, satiny complexions. Both men and women favour a style of decorative scarification, which raises the skin of chest, stomach and face in remarkable patterns of bumps and cicatrices. Other forms of personal ornamentation include heavy bone bangles, bright bead necklaces and spikes of ivory or brass thrust through a hole pierced in the lower lip and protruding down over the chin. Maidens bathing naked in the river sometimes pause, entranced, to admire their reflections with innocent narcissism — for the paraphernalia of modern vanity are rare in these parts. The traveller who brings presents of mirrors or other simple trinkets to the Nuer will find himself surrounded by willing takers. Even cast-off empty film boxes or soup packets have a value and are quickly snatched up from the ground to be woven into necklaces or hung from a piece of string as pendants.

For the urbanised visitor, a day spent among the Nuer constitutes an unforgettable experience. Modern Western man, with his extreme sophistication, his technological know-how and, let it be said, his cares and worries engendered by the frenetic pace of late-20th century life, here finds his exact polar opposite — a people whose mode of existence is as slow, timeless and unchanging as the river that flows through their land. Bright-eyed, intelligent and endlessly curious, the Nuer are very far from meriting that ill-judged epithet 'primitive'; but theirs, undoubtedly, is a simple culture, uncomplicated by the need to adapt to rapid changes and uncluttered by the pressures, phobias and anxieties of the modern world. It is a mistake either to scorn or to idealise such a culture — better just to accept it for what it is and to be glad that our world is still wide enough to accommodate such simplicity.

To these gentle, charming people, the traveller appearing suddenly around a bend of the Baro in his mud-spattered Landrover must appear

Right: Anuak family compound stands in the shade of mango trees, beneath which women sit nursing children, talking and smoking pipes of heady aromatic tobacco.

every bit as strange and exotic as they do to him. Pitch your tent by the edge of a village and the Nuer will flock out to welcome you and to examine you with undisguised fascination — first the children, then young men and women, and finally the elders. Pale complexions and fair hair are still an extreme novelty here and much exploratory touching and prodding goes on, as though to determine that you are not, in fact, just a figment of the collective imagination. But in the midst of a dense press of giggling girls and solemn serious-faced young men, you will not for a moment feel threatened or overwhelmed — rather, the encounter produces a mood of calm introspection that quiets the troubled mind and leaves you at peace with yourself and with your surroundings. The Nuer and the Westerner, two peoples from different ends of the earth, and from the far extremes of the cultural continuum, here discover to their mutual delight that, despite their superficial dissimilarities, they do indeed have much in common, much to share, much to give each other.

In the evenings, as the sun drops low in the sky over the Baro, the Nuer bring in their scattered herds from grazing grounds on the surrounding plains, to camps established on the banks of the river. Nuer love of their cattle is legendary and is often expressed in poems and songs of great beauty extolling the virtues of favourite beasts — whole verses may be devoted to intricate and lyrical description of the curve of a horn, the moulding of a hoof or the particular shade of a hide. As dusk falls over the cattle camp and the herds return, each animal is tethered for the night to its own individual peg — which it knows and goes to automatically. The setting sun picks out and illustrates a medley of silhouettes — tall guards standing one-legged leaning on spears, women trudging up from the river with water, proud bulls with long lyre-shaped horns and the beehive profiles of huts. Smoke from innumerable camp-fires spirals up to mingle with the gathering darkness, and the air is filled with voices raised in laughter and song.

The Nuer are only one amongst many of Ethiopia's cattle herding peoples; indeed, throughout most of the country's lowland areas pastoralism is the predominant lifestyle, and settled agriculture is either impossible or despised. If this is true in general of the people who live along the Baro towards Ethiopia's western border with the Sudan, it is even more true, 300 kilometres or so as the crow flies to the south and east, of the inhabitants of the Omo River basin who follow their herds across the endless savannah lands between Ethiopia and Kenya.

The Omo, one of Ethiopia's longest rivers, never reaches the sea. It flows instead into Lake Turkana in northern Kenya after a journey of almost 1,000 kilometres from the central highland escarpment. Reckoned by enthusiasts to be Africa's premier location for the sport of white

water river-rafting, its early fury takes it through gorges hundreds of metres deep and over formidable cataracts; thence it snakes more peacefully through dense jungles and finally across colourful desert terrain. Its waters boil with fish and the huge shapes of crocodiles and hippopotami.

In the far south, near the Kenya border, the Omo provides the line of demarcation between the Ethiopian regions of Kaffa to the west, and Gamo Gofa to the east. Because of the giant herds of plains game that still wander in this area and because of its unique ecology, two important national parks have quite recently been established here — Omo in Kaffa and Mago in Gamo Gofa. Both offer incredible spectacles of oryx, giraffe, zebra, hartebeest, gerenuk and gazelle, as well as lion, buffalo and elephant. Both have the merit, also, of being far from the beaten track, and virtually unexplored, and thus are places in which game can be seen in a truly natural state, undisturbed by the depredations of man. Of the two however, Mago, on the east bank of the river, is the most remote and remains wholly uncommercialised — a characteristic which the Government of Ethiopia intends to preserve. In the dense acacia scrub of the park itself, close to the river, and in the broad rolling grasslands and deserts that surround it, the traveller enters a lost world, across which few vehicles have ever travelled and which few foreign eyes have ever seen.

So vast are the horizons beneath the blue and pitiless sky, so scattered are the signs of any kind of human habitation, so few are the landmarks, that it is extremely easy to become disoriented here, to lose contact with the roughly north-to-south flow of the river, and to become marooned in an endless sea of waving savannah grass. The wise traveller, like a sailor on the ocean, carries a compass, as well as generous supplies of food, water and fuel. Even thus equipped, the driving conditions can be so difficult, and any sense of direction can become so seriously misled, that the only hope of salvation for those who become lost may lie in recruiting the services of one of the occasional pastoral herdsmen who wander here with their cattle to act as a guide and a deliverer. Totally at home in this wilderness, the nomads of the southern Omo basin have evolved a strategy of survival that enables them to live successfully in an environment which, despite its lulling natural beauty, can also be a hostile, deadly and implacable foe. Intricate knowledge of the terrain and of the places in which water can be found, coupled with an infallible navigational sense, makes it possible for these handsome, proud and independent folk to sustain themselves and even to extract a modicum of prosperity — measured in cattle, sheep and goats — from a land into which few others dare to venture. The people of the Omo — the Karo,

Above: Herd of dun-coloured hartebeest crosses the grassy savannah of the Omo basin. Littered with the wierd shapes of giant termite hills, this is a lost world across which few vehicles have ever travelled, and which few foreign eyes have seen.

the Galeb, the Bume, the Amer, the Bena and others — are the distant relatives of the Oromo people of central Ethiopia. Their languages, classed by scholars as 'Omotic' represent a southwards and westwards extension of the Cushitic family of tongues — although here the gutturals of Oromo are considerably softened, and the overall cadences of speech take on a more lyrical sing-song quality. The deep structure of grammar, however, remains the same, as do many aspects of vocabulary — for example the number 'two', which in Oromo is 'lame' and in the Omotic tongues 'lane' or 'lena'. The nomadic lifestyle itself is another connecting factor and the small hand-carried stools, also used as pillows to support the neck, that pastoralists in the Omo valley keep with them on their wanderings, are also seen amongst the Borana Oromo in the Sidamo lowlands far to the east. Here in the Omo, however, the Islamic faith of the Borana has not penetrated and the vast majority of the people are pagans, worshipping the old gods of the Horn of Africa — the sun and the moon and the spirits that reside in trees and rocks.

North from the shores of Lake Turkana as far as Jinka, westwards to

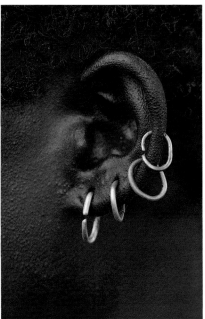

Below: Multiple earrings are a typical male decoration amongst the peoples of the Omo.

Left: Viewed through gaps in the wattle-and-daub walls of a village hut, two Amer girls demonstrate their love of elaborate beads and bracelets, and of ochre-plastered hairstyles.

Above: Girl of the Omo valley with colourful bead necklaces, headband and blue plastic earrings. Female vanity finds many different and inventive forms of expression in this tough semi-desert region.

Left: Amer girls wearing cowrie-shell necklaces and headbands decorated with large oval plates of beaten tin.

Below: Earrings, a feather head-dress and a skull-cap of dried red mud are all popular forms of personal decoration amongst the men of the Omo valley.

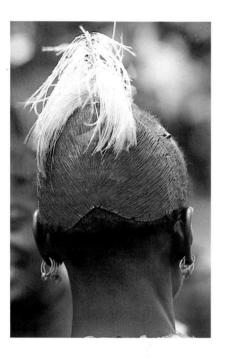

the borders of the Sudan, and east as far as Lake Chew Bahir, the Omotic peoples form a distinct community, isolated from the rest of Ethiopia by the formidable environment in which they live. Clothing styles for men are simple in the extreme, ranging from nothing at all amongst the Bume, the Karo and the Galeb who live along both banks of the Omo north of Kalam and Omorati, to plain wrap-around cloths and togas amongst the Amer and Bena. Multiple earrings are a popular male decoration, as are elaborate hairstyles shaped and sculptured with razors, smoothed flat at the front of the head with a skull-cap of dried red mud, and often topped of with an ostrich feather. Women are even more extravagantly coiffured with their hair in ochre-plastered ringlets or, amongst the Amer, wearing headbands decorated with large oval plates of burnished tin. Generally naked from-the waist up, the women of this region wear short knee-length leather skirts, the hems of which are decorated and weighed down with many jingling iron nails beaten into rings. Female vanity is also expressed in capes and headdresses fringed with cowrie shells, metal bracelets worn around the ankles and wrists, and elaborate gaudy necklaces.

Although predominantly pastoralists, some of the peoples of the Omo valley who live closest to the river itself have adopted a mixed economy that includes hunting and gathering, and some sorghum cultivation. At Doose, the Karo have established a substantial village, and cultivate the fertile river banks. And at Kangateen — midway between Omorati and Jinka, the Bume seem to have given up pastoralism altogether, depending for their living instead upon hunting — carried out by large parties of men on foot — in the game-rich plains to the east. Fishing is conducted from long, highly unstable dug-out canoes which the villagers also use to ferry themselves across the muddy, crocodile-infested waters of the Omo, punting upstream and then drifting down on the current to the desired landing point. It is the pastoral lifestyle, however, that remains the hallmark of this region. The tough wandering herdsmen, armed with old carbines or spears to fend off predators, alone with their cattle amidst the limitless sweep of the savannah, constitute an unforgettable image of the dignity, independence and resourcefulness of humankind.

The Omo valley is an extension of the Great Ethiopian Rift, the colossal volcanic scar that runs the entire length of the country from north to south. This remarkable geological feature undergoes many changes of altitude and terrain on its journey, and the first of these changes becomes apparent to the traveller about 100 kilometres to the east of the Omo beyond Lake Chew Bahir. Here the savannah and scrub begin gradually to merge into low hills covered with terracing, regular irrigation

Opposite: Bume fishermen work from long, highly unstable dug-out canoes — also used as ferries across the muddy, crocodile-infested waters of the Omo.

channels and the soft lush green of crops. The point where the rugged individualistic culture of the nomad gives way to the more staid and settled ethnic of the lifelong farmer is known as Konso, after the people who live here. Cultivators for centuries, the Konso, like the Omotics to the west and south, are speakers of a Cushitic language; however it is a language much more closely related to the mainstream Oromo that the traveller will encounter with increasing frequency as he continues his journey through the Rift.

The Konso have adopted a complex age-grading system (also found in different variations among the Borana and among other Oromo nationalities). The first age-grade accommodates all male children from, roughly, six to 12; at adolescence they move into a new stratum that prepares them for manhood; thence into the warrior class, prosperous land-owning middle-age and, finally, to the exalted position of elders. Each grade has its own communal 'club-house', and a special large central building in all villages, open at the sides, with a dome-shaped thatched roof, acts as the sleeping quarters for all unmarried boys and young men. A pagan society, the Konso erect eerie wooden totems replete with phallic symbols over the graves of the dead, and have numerous cults based around the breeding and veneration of serpents. Sacred drums, symbolising peace and harmony, are circulated from village to village according to a fixed cycle and are beaten in rituals that mark the transition from one age-grade to the next.

The keynote of Konso culture, however, is a highly specialised and successful agricultural economy that, through terracing buttressed with stone, enables these people to extract a productive living from the none-too-fertile hills and valleys that surround them. So extensive and so intricate has this system of terracing become that, at first sight, it seems as though a giant comb has sculpted and coiffured the contours into abstract patterns of curves and spirals. The stone shoring employed in the terraces finds its echoes in the dry-stone walls that surround most Konso villages and that protect low-lying fields from flash-floods and marauding cattle. Stone, used also for grinding grain, sharpening knives and spears, making anvils and constructing dams is, as one writer has observed, "as much a part of Konso life as soil. Their use of stone gives clarity and definition to their towns and homesteads which is extremely striking to the observer; it conveys a sense of harmony, order and industry, and is in these respects a true expression of their values."

Konso industriousness finds its vehicle in a cooperative ethic that enables each farmer to enlist the support of communal work parties from his own and surrounding villages to build walls and terraces, and to sow and harvest the principal crops — sorghum, potatoes and cotton. Konso

Above: Bume hunter, his rifle held loosely and a pack of fresh slaughtered meat strapped to his back, returning to his village.

Below: Konso grave totems, despite their 'modern' shelter of corrugated iron sheeting, still appear weird and unearthly. A pagan society, the Konso have a well organised social structure and are renowned for their agricultural skills.

weaving, also a communal activity, is highly productive and the thick cotton blankets for which this region is famous are much prized throughout Ethiopia. Not all of Konso life, however, is dominated by hard work, and evening is a particular time of relaxation. Then, the young men and girls sing and dance to a hypnotic stamping rhythm, forming fluid circles and squares punctuated with much provocative shaking of the hips and breasts and with warlike leaps and bounds.

Konso country, green and densely farmed, provides the ecological dividing line between the dry and austere Omo plains to the west and south and the lush environment of Ethiopia's seven Rift Valley lakes which extend northwards from here in a long chain that stops not far short of Addis Ababa. Out of Konso, the road through Gamo Gofa province leads, like a deliverer from the wilderness, to the town of Arba Minch perched on a hillside overlooking the picturesque plinth of thickly forested land which separates Lake Chamo from Lake Abaya, the southernmost two of the Rift Valley family. Gazing out over this lovely causeway, locally known as 'the Bridge of Heaven', the traveller surveys a landscape in every respect different from that of the terrain through which he has passed on the journey from the Omo River, and is reminded once again of the recurrent theme of contrast and sudden transition lying at the heart of the symphony of sight, sound and cultural experience that is Ethiopia.

Chapter Four · The Lakes and the Valley

Arba Minch, the regional capital of Gamo Gofa, 505 kilometres south-west of Addis Ababa, is a rapidly growing, fast modernising town that enjoys electricity 24 hours a day, fairly good telephone links with other regions, a well-equipped hospital, a small airport, and an excellent — if rather quaint — hotel that commands splendid views of both Lake Chamo and Lake Abaya and of the Nechisar National Park that embraces their eastern shores. Entry to Nech Sar is afforded by a winding track through the forest of trees and brush that adorns the Bridge of Heaven, the narrow hilly promontory between the two lakes. The high, grassy plains beyond support the last remnants of a once-extensive population of Swayne's hartebeest — a species of large antelope that is endemic to Ethiopia — as well as herds of zebra and Grant's gazelle.

Arba Minch means in Amharic 'Forty Springs' and, indeed, at least this many springs do rise in the jungle on the west side of the Bridge of Heaven, directly below the town. The spring waters, which feed a series of streams, are ice-cold and crystal clear and, when cupped in the hand or in one of the large lily leaves that grow round about, take on the sheen of quicksilver, reflecting the light that arches down through the canopy of leaves above with a transitory mercurial beauty.

The main feature of the region however, which makes a most enduring impression on the mind of the visitor, is constituted by the lakes themselves — for Chamo and Abaya, the members of the Rift Valley family that stand closest to the great south-western Ethiopian wilderness, still have about them an aura of primal savagery and untamed grandeur despite the development that has recently been initiated at Arba Minch. The waters of the two lakes are alive with tigerfish, catfish, tilapia and giant Nile perch weighing up to 100 kilogrammes. Avifauna includes colonies of bright yellow weaver birds thousands strong, four brilliantly coloured species of kingfisher, Great White pelicans, storks, ibises, spoonbills and fish eagles. Waterbuck and leopard inhabit the Bridge of Heaven, and the hoarse coughing roar of lions can be heard at night from the gardens of the hotel, mingled with the laugh of the hyena and the high-pitched song of cicadas. Lake Chamo also has several large herds of hippopotamus, and the muddy promontories of its reed-lined shores and islands provide basking grounds for countless hundreds of Nile crocodile, some of which reach colossal proportions of 10 metres or so from nose to tail. Launching themselves into the water with terrifying speed and strength as soon as they pick up the vibrations of an approaching boat, these prehistoric titans had arrived at the perfect limits of their evolutionary specialisation 200 million years ago. Faultless killing machines, their species has not found it necessary to adapt or change to the slightest degree since the era in which their long-extinct

Opposite: The flat rolling grasslands of Nechisar National Park, on the eastern shores of Lakes Abaya and Chamo, are a haven for large herds of zebra and other plains game.

Above: The '40 springs' which have given the town of Arba Minch its name, produce sweet, clear and ice-cold water which shimmers like mercury when it catches the light.

Opposite: The green banks of Lake Chamo are the basking grounds for thousands of monstrous Nile crocodiles. Some, like this giant, reach lengths of 10 metres or more.

relatives, the dinosaurs, walked the earth. It is an eerie, spine-chilling and undeniably dangerous adventure to guide a small boat into their midst. Long reptilian snouts, topped by small beady red eyes that gaze at the visitor with an evil and unblinking intensity, protrude above water-level and, all around, sinuous swirls and eddies mark the lash and sweep of the powerful tails that provide the main source of locomotion for these deadly saurians, as they hunt in the muddy and impenetrable deep.

Chamo, with a surface area of 551 square kilometres, and Abaya, which extends to 1,160 square kilometres, are, by a considerable margin, the largest of Ethiopia's Rift Valley lakes. Both are areas of dramatic scenic beauty with many islands and secluded peninsulas that the setting sun picks out and silhouettes in shades of burnished gold and purple as it declines over the eastern shores. The quiet waters reflect the last light of the day with a mirror-like intensity as the stars come out, and then a cooling evening breeze sighs across the still surface, breaking it into ripples and wavelets that extend in all directions as far as the eye can see.

Despite the ample opportunities for fishing that lakes Chamo and Abaya afford, very few of the people living around the shores are full-time fishermen. Instead, agriculture — promoted by well-watered alluvial soils on which virtually anything that is planted will grow — is the majority occupation, with the principal crops being barley, maize, sorghum, coffee, tobacco and cotton. There is also an established tradition of weaving in small cottage industries that brings in welcome additional income and adds colour to the local scene.

The inhabitants of the southern Rift Valley zone are a remarkable medley of many of the 80 or more ethnic groups of which Ethiopia is composed — particularly since resettlement and relocation of Amhara and other northern peoples has taken place here in recent years, and since the region is on the historic path of the western and northwards migration of the Oromo.

Perhaps the most interesting community to the visitor, however, are the indigenous Dorze, once a warrior people but now exclusively farmers and weavers who fashion beautiful *shammas* — the colourful toga-like garment worn by many Ethiopian men and women — from locally grown cotton. Dorze are found in great numbers as far south as Arba Minch, but their traditional homeland is located somewhat further north, around the town of Chencha, in the 4,000-metre-high Guge range of mountains that overlook the western shores of Lake Abaya.

A steep winding track leads up from the left of the main north road out of Arba Minch into the Guge mountains. Here, in the space of a 26-kilometre drive from the lakeside, the traveller will see unfolding before him some of the many changes of vegetation cover and climate that are

Below left: The Dorze people are famous throughout Ethiopia for the quality and beauty of the woven cotton. Working on simple handlooms, and moving with blinding speed, they can produce up to nine metres of cloth a day.
Below: A Dorze man sewing together two lengths of fine cotton to make a shamma, *the shawl-like garment worn by all Ethiopians*

152

Below: A friendly press of people greets the visitor who stops at a roadside market.

Bottom: Small children, laden with fruit for sale, at one of the busy roadside markets in southern Ethiopia.

possible in Ethiopia between lowland and highland zones. The lush tropical trees of the valley floor quickly give way to thickets of bamboo and then to scattered juniper forests draped with Spanish moss. The air becomes cool, almost cold, and patches of mist hug the ground, at times indistinguishable from the cloud banks that descend over the tallest peaks.

It is here, in this rarefied alpine atmosphere, that the unique traditional houses of the Dorze first begin to appear in villages clustered by the side of the road up to Chencha and beyond. Built by skilled and experienced carpenters, these towering structures have no parallel in Ethiopia. Standing 12 or more metres high, they are shaped like enormous beehives, the smooth convex curve of the continuous roof and walls only being broken at the front of the building where a 'nose'-like doorway, furnished with two benches, acts as an entrance and reception room for guests. The spacious sleeping and living quarters beyond are cool and dark, with floors of compacted earth, and have an airy feel produced by the vaulted ceiling and walls which are thatched with *ensete* (false

Below: Tall Dorze home with its prominent nose-shaped entrance. Made from bamboo (cut only on moolit nights) and thatched with false banana leaves, the structure — sometimes over 12 metres high — can last up to 40 years before their owners finally abandon them.

banana) fronds stretched over a complicated bamboo frame. Each house, in its own stockaded garden, is surrounded by other slightly lower structures of the same design which fulfil specialised functions — one might be a cow byre, another a kitchen, a third a 'guest cottage', a fourth a workshop. Unusual in the Ethiopian countryside, Dorze houses are durable structures that often last their owners for 40 years or more.

And if the lower part of the wall is attacked by termites or starts to rot, a family's home can simply be uprooted from the ground and carried on poles to another location, there to be trimmed and re-established, slightly shorter than before.

Returning from the mountains around Chencha, the traveller will enjoy breathtaking views over precipitous slopes that tumble down to the platinum waters of Lake Abaya and, rejoining the main northbound road at the lake's edge, will find himself again surrounded by the thick green forests of the fertile lowlands. Here, in clearings in the jungle, numerous villages begin to appear from which bright-eyed laughing children run out to offer mangoes, bananas, oranges and limes at give-away prices. Towards the northern end of the lake, however, where the regional boundary is crossed from Gamo Gofa into the productive north-western corner of what was Sidamo Province, a subtle change of terrain is encountered as black cotton soil is replaced by red laterite clay overplanted with fields of yellow maize and the bright metallic green of coffee bushes.

The first main town that the traveller passes through is Sodo, which stands on high ground overlooking the Rift Valley from an altitude of 2,100 metres. An important marketing centre for the region as a whole, Sodo has an almost exclusively Oromo population and has expanded enormously in recent years with the construction of a series of good roads linking it to neighbouring provinces and to Addis Ababa, 379 kilometres to the north. Westwards from Sodo, the great central escarpment stretches away into Kaffa province, the home of Ethiopian coffee and, indeed, the first home of all the coffee in the world.

The drink was taken from here to Yemen in the 14th century, where it acquired its Arabic name *qahweh* — possibly a colloquialisation of 'Kaffa', soon converted to *kahveh* in Turkish, *caffe* in Italian, *Kaffee* in German, café in French and *koffie* in Dutch. It was the Dutch who ensured the onward propagation of coffee from Yemen, taking seedlings to Indonesia towards the end of the 17th century. French and British traders completed the process, establishing plantations all over the world.

Legends as to the actual discovery of coffee are numerous, but perhaps the most attractive is that of the 'dancing goats'. According to tradition, Kaldi, a young Ethiopian goat-herd from Kaffa, was surprised that his lazy and sleepy charges became suddenly invigorated and began to prance about excitedly after chewing certain berries. He tried the berries himself and found them stimulating — indeed in large enough quantities they produced a mood of merriness akin to intoxication. The legend has it that a monk from one of the many monasteries nearby came upon Kaldi in this happy state and decided to try the berries too. That night, during an arduous session of prayer, he discovered that he remained wide awake with his mind more active and acute than it normally was on these occasions. Accordingly he passed on the coffee secret to the brothers of his order and soon all the monks in Ethiopia were chewing the berries, rendering up their devotions without the troublesome interference of sleep.

For many centuries after its discovery, coffee was eaten and not drunk. Berries were either taken whole, or crushed and mixed with ghee (clarified butter) — a practice that still persists in the remoter regions of former Kaffa and Sidamo to this day. Later refinements included a

156

The ensete *plant is painstakingly cared for; each tree of a specific age has its own particular hole in the ground, and as it matures it is moved nearer the house until, when it is about 10 years old, it is cut down. The fronds and fibres are used for house-building and rope. The huge vegetative bulb is dug up, pounded and then stored in holes in the ground where it is left to ferment and then baked into the grey waffle-like bread of the Guraghe people. Perched, like a spider in a web, opposite, a housebuilder supervises his assistants in the construction of what will be the steep thatched roof of a Guraghe home.*

158

variety of wine made with fermented pulp and another concoction produced from the dried fruit and beans. It was not until the 13th century that the practice of brewing a hot drink from roasted beans was introduced, but this soon acquired a widespread popularity. In Ethiopia today the whole elaborate process — pounding of the beans, roasting them on a slightly concave iron plate over a shallow charcoal brazier, adding cloves and other spices, brewing in pots of hot water, and finally, pouring out into tiny china cups — has taken on the trappings of a ritual in which the aroma of coffee mingles with the heady scent of incense. Here the traveller may enjoy 'the world's favourite drink' with a flavour that is far superior to the 'instant' brands displayed on the supermarket shelves of Europe and America — a flavour much enhanced by the ceremonial surroundings.

In parts of Kaffa wild coffee bushes still grow in much the same state as Kaldi, the happy goat-herd, must have found them so many centuries ago. The province, centred on its large regional capital of Jimma (about 100 kilometres in a straight line north-west of Sodo and 335 kilometres south-west of Addis Ababa), provides almost perfect conditions for the plant. Its rolling hillsides and valleys, at altitudes from 2,100 metres down to 1,300 metres, receive just the right amount of rainfall — 1,500 to 2,500 millimetres a year — and have slightly acidic topsoils with pH values between 4.5 and 5.5. The people, too, have an established tradition of coffee cultivation, today harnessed to numerous cooperatives and to highly productive farms that make Ethiopia one of the world's leading exporters of highest-quality *Arabicas*.

Eastwards and north from Jimma, which is Ethiopia's most important coffee-collecting centre, a good road runs through a highland zone of great scenic beauty, climbing up a mountainside, descending into the valley of the Omo river (which here, near its headwaters, is known as the Ghibe), and then rising again to the edge of the great plateau which, between Welkite, Indibir and Hosaana, offers dramatic views of the Great Rift Valley with its necklace of lakes.

The area bounded by Welkite in the north, Hosaana in the south and the plunge into the Rift to the east, has, for many hundreds of years, been the homeland of one of Ethiopia's most remarkable and industrious peoples — the Guraghe. Of mixed Semitic and Hamitic stock, it is probable that they migrated here from further north in the long-forgotten past. But wherever they came from originally, they have made themselves at home here in the southern highlands, and have evolved a uniquely vigorous and self-reliant economy.

The basis of this economy is the false banana tree, known throughout Ethiopia as ensete. Its cycle of growth determines the rhythm and special

Below: The ritual of the coffee ceremony in the gardens of Addis Ababa's Hilton Hotel. Accompanied by burning incense the coffee is roasted, ground and brewed with spices over a charcoal brazier.

nature of the Guraghe lifestyle, providing both their staple foodstuff and the materials from which their homes are constructed. Each house, tall and spacious with a high thatched roof, stands in its own garden of up to 10 hectares. Around the house are rows of *ensete* trees, the youngest plants further away followed by increasingly older and taller layers radiating inwards. Specific holes are reserved for trees of a specific age and the plants are rotated from hole to hole as they mature until, at the age of eight to 10 years, they are ready to be cut down. The bark and fibres of the felled tree are taken away to be used for building and rope-making, and the massive vegetative bulb is dug up, shredded, and then reburied, wrapped in leaves in a new line of holes close to the house. Here it ferments into a thick cheesy paste which the Guraghe use, in unleavened form, to bake into the grey, sour-flavoured waffle bread that constitutes the basis of their diet.

Beyond the ensete plantation most Guraghe farmers grow cash crops including coffee, *khat* (a mild stimulant popular in many parts of eastern Ethiopia), tobacco, and eucalyptus trees (for firewood). These crops all produce substantial revenues for the Guraghe who, rendered self-sufficient for their staple food by the wonderful properties of the ensete, often become extremely prosperous. This prosperity is reflected in their well-furnished circular houses, which are supported by an imposing central mainstay, and are divided within into sleeping, living and cooking areas, with a large section to one side where the family's cattle and goats are kept. Mats and carpets cover the earth floor of the main living quarters, colourful baskets hang in precise rows along the walls, and beautifully-fashioned pottery is arranged around the hearth.

A mixed community of Muslims and Christians, the Guraghe live in what must surely be one of the pleasantest parts of Ethiopia. Reminiscent of the idyllic images of rural life produced by the English painter Constable in the 19th century, their villages stand surrounded by grassy commons and meadows where horses graze beside thatched dwellings and where carpenters prepare the wicker frames of new homes. Beneath blue skies, the fresh invigorating air has a peculiar clarity that enables the traveller gazing eastwards over the edge of the Rift, from the road that runs south along the escarpment connecting Indibir with Hosaana, to see for more than 100 kilometres across the valley floor to the foothills of the Bale Mountain range. Between the two escarpments, and far below, lie the glittering watery jewels of Lake Awasa, Lake Shala, Lake Abyata, Lake Langano and Lake Ziway, Ethiopia's Rift Valley riviera.

Ziway, the northernmost of these five lakes, lies only about 160 kilometres from Addis Ababa and is consequently rather popular with day-trippers from the capital. With a surface area of 447 square

kilometres, it has a maximum depth of about 15 metres. Oval in shape and studded with islands, it has marshy shores, overgrown with reeds, that provide an ideal habitat for storks, pelicans, wild ducks, geese and fish eagles, as well as for hippopotami in great numbers.

Further south, at a distance of some 200 kilometres from Addis Ababa, Lake Langano has been developed as a major holiday and recreation centre well equipped for water sports. With a circumference of 82 kilometres, it reaches a depth of 30 metres in places and has several large and pleasant bays edged with sandy beaches. The mountains to the east of Langano provide a lovely stage behind which the morning sun rises in a panoply of rich colours.

Roughly parallel with Langano, but on the western side of the main north-south road, is Lake Abyata — justly the most famous for its birdlife of all the Rift Valley family. This is a shallow lake, reaching a maximum depth of only 10 metres, and it lies in a gracefully-cured basin of land set amidst low hills. Its alkaline waters attract flamingos in their thousands — shy birds that, at any human approach, rise from their feeding grounds along the shore into brilliant pink and red flight. Like a congregation of conservative church-goers outraged by a daring sermon, they depart ponderously to a safe distance, honking and clucking their disapproval. Other bird species include wild geese and cormorants, Marabou storks and Sacred ibises.

Great White pelicans, too, feed off the plentiful fish stocks of Lake Abyata in daylight hours, but these birds return for the night to their island breeding grounds in nearby Lake Shala, a little to the south. With a surface area of 409 square kilometres, Lake Shala reaches colossal depths of up to 250 metres and is rimmed round with jagged peaks and imposing rock formations that give it a rather strange and mysterious air. In the south-west corner of the lake is the mouth of a small stream that winds back into the hills under a canopy of giant wild fig trees, euphorbia and acacias. Here, tall Oromo herdsmen, with the handsome dignified bearing of Biblical patriarchs, bring their cattle down to graze in surroundings of pastoral tranquillity. Armed with sturdy wicked-bladed spears to fend off predators, these people have adhered to the nomadic lifestyle that much of the rest of the Oromo people elsewhere in Ethiopia have long since abandoned.

South again from Lake Shala, at a distance of 275 kilometres from Addis Ababa, lies Lake Awasa, the smallest link in the Rift Valley chain, but also the prettiest. Reaching a depth of 21 metres, the lake has a circumference of 62 kilometres with reed-lined shores and many swampy bays. Its waters teem with fish including barbus, perch, tilapia and catfish in great numbers. A fair-sized local fishing community

Opposite: Moments before a storm breaks, a rainbow shimmers above the tiny village of Yayi, where horses graze on the common.

Right: Young girl at Awasa market, her hair decorated with cowrie shells and beads.

Opposite: Horses burdened with wood cross the vast green expanse of the rolling moorlands of Bale, and in the distance the mountains rise into blue and grey.

using small boats and simple nets and lures thrives on these stocks, as do many species of birds — storks and herons in particular which can be seen wading watchfully in the shallows on their long thin angular legs. Kingfishers, darters, plovers, wild ducks, Egyptian geese, crakes and cormorants add to the colourful spectacle.

The town of Awasa is the capital of the former province of Sidamo and supports a large open market to which the inhabitants of this region, both settled and nomadic, bring their produce to sell and barter. Cattle, goats and chickens here are traded alongside lemons, tomatoes, green peppers, pungent spices, grains, sugar cane, and country butter wrapped in banana leaves. News from outlying areas is another hot commodity and, as they gather to gossip, the Sidama and Oromo peoples of Ethiopia can be seen in all their remarkable variety, women and girls outdoing one another in the splendour of their silver and brass jewellery and the elaborate sculpturing of their hairstyles.

Eastwards from Awasa, through the boom town of Shashamene (which has grown by an estimated 4,000 per cent in the last 30 years as a result of the rich agriculture-based commerce of this region) a dry-weather road runs up into the mountains of the neighbouring province of Bale — an area of great natural beauty. Here the warm climate and dense cultivation of the Rift Valley floor are left behind and expanses of emerald green rolling moorland open out, interspersed with isolated settlements.

Predominantly populated by Oromos, Bale appears to lie at the heart of the original homeland of these people and was the seat of their traditional high priests in times gone by. Although there was much early conversion to Islam, ancient pagan practices resisted total obliteration and can still be seen expressed today in the tall megalithic gravestones, carved with human and animal figures, that mark the burial places of important personages. Similarly, although largely Muslim, the women of this region reflect older customs in their style of clothing. They do not veil their faces, wearing instead a handsome black headdress drawn up into a wimple over the forehead and hanging down behind over the neck and shoulders where it is often decorated with bright tassels of green or yellow cotton.

The main means of getting from place to place in this cool upland country is still the horse. Both men and women ride, galloping across the moors with the haughty upright posture of a warrior race. Cattle herding and dairy farming are the principal sources of livelihood, coupled with an expanding timber industry that draws on the huge expanses of forest that bedeck the Bale mountainsides. Here, as the land rises through 3,000 metres to 4,000 metres and more, scenery is revealed reminiscent of the

Simien range far to the north. Giant St John's wort and heather appear, red-hot pokers sprout brilliantly from the hillsides, and parasitic Spanish moss drips from the branches of tall junipers.

On the high plateau between the 4,307-metre summit of Mount Batu to the south and the village of Dinshu to the north, the Bale Mountains National Park has been established as the last main refuge in Ethiopia of the rare Mountain nyala and of the Simien red fox (much more common here than in the region from which it takes its name). Thirteen of Ethiopia's 23 endemic bird species are also found here, and the park has many superb fishing streams well stocked with brown and rainbow trout.

Beyond Dinshu, the road through Bale passes Goba, the regional capital, which stands at an altitude of 2,500 metres, surrounded by looming peaks, some 430 kilometres from Addis Ababa. Thence, the terrain drops steadily towards the east and alpine flora and fauna are replaced by red sandy plains covered with acacias. Horses give way to camels as beasts of burden and the nomadic lifestyle, that everywhere

Opposite and overleaf: The river Weyb, which flows into the Sof Omar caves, has, over thousands of years, cut a maze of passages and galleries, silent chambers and airy vaults, and high fluted archways, into the white limestone.

else dominates in the Ethiopian lowlands, reasserts itself.

Here, 120 kilometres or so east of Goba, lost in a low valley amidst thorn trees and the weird funnels of termite hills, the Weyb River flows into a giant underground cave system that, with its arched portals, high eroded ceilings and deep, vaulted, echoing chambers lives up to — and perhaps surpasses — the opium-inspired visions of Coleridge in his haunting poem *Kublai Khan*. These caves, now an important Islamic shrine named after the saintly Sheikh Sof Omar who took refuge here many centuries ago, have a religious history that, in fact, predates the arrival of the Muslims in Bale — a history calibrated in thousands, not hundreds, of years. The first religions of this part of Africa revolved around spirit worship and ghost-cults in which the most powerful supernatural beings were believed to attach themselves to trees, rocks, and most forcefully, to caves, which became places of veneration where prayers were offered up and sacrifices made. Despite the superficial and comparatively recent veneer of Islam, the visitor to Sof Omar will see many signs of the persistence of such pagan beliefs and practices: a group of men sacrificing a goat; tokens of leather and cloth hung from rocky projections within the cave. There is an atmosphere of hushed, numinous dread about the whole area which is a fertile breeding ground for superstition, and which even the most detached atheist cannot contemplate without feelings of mysterious, irrational awe.

The approach to the caves is made through the tiny village of Sof Omar, perched on the cliffs above the Weyb River. Here black-faced Vervet monkeys play and chatter amongst the rocks, well tolerated by the local people who go about their business of tending the shrine and providing for pilgrims with a slow pace of ritual and ceremony that seems as timeless and enduring as the earth itself. To the rear of the village is a dark gaping crevice down which a precipitous narrow footpath winds to the floor of the first cave. Only a few patches of sunlight filter into this dimly-lit kingdom, which extends away in all directions through vast subterranean passageways of polished white limestone, carved by the flood and recess of the river over countless ages. In this process nature has worked a marvel of architecture — soaring pillars of stone 20 metres high, flying buttresses dwarfing those that support the cathedral of Notre Dame, fluted archways and tall airy vaults. Silence is the visitor's constant companion, broken only by the subdued echo of his footsteps and the soft susurration of water trickling down the cavern walls and splashing into cool dark pools. Finally, the river itself is reached, a sunless sea flowing through a deep gorge, going on almost two kilometres underground before breaking through into the day again.

The countryside around the Sof Omar caves abounds with wildlife — dik-dik and kudu, serval cats, rock hyraxes, giant tortoises, snakes and lizards, and more than 50 species of birds. It is here, too, that the true plains of Ethiopia begin as the land gradually collapses towards the east. A journey of 150 kilometres takes the traveller to Imi, the point where Bale merges into Harerghe, Ethiopia's largest region. Here, across the endless red wastes of the savannah, in a landscape dotted with a million termite hills, Somali-speaking nomads wander with their herds of camels and cattle following the sparse rains to transitory pastures. Eastwards, towards Kebre Dehar and Warder, dust, wind and the baking heat of the merciless midday sun create an environment where only the strong and cunning survive.

Though Harerghe is largely a land of desert and low-lying savannah, its northern reaches are mountainous and fertile and it is here, on the high edge of the eastern Ethiopian escarpment that Harar, the capital, is located. This medieval walled city, with its more than 90 mosques and shrines, is considered the fourth most sacred centre of the Islamic world.

Right: The Grand Mosque at Harar has two whitewashed minarets which dominate a broad courtyard where pilgrims cleanse themselves in preparation for prayer.

172

Established in 1520 by a local chief, Sultan Abu Bakr Muhammad, Harar shortly afterwards was besieged and captured by the fanatical Muslim leader, Ahmed Gragn, who used it as a headquarters from which to launch his devastating *jihad* against the Christian Ethiopian kingdom to the west.

After each expedition in this holy war, Gragn's soldiers returned to Harar, as his chronicler claims, "victorious, triumphant and happy". They brought back extensive booty, including cattle, horses and other livestock, swords, coats-of-mail and weapons of all sorts, a large amount of gold and silver, many silks and costly clothes, and a vast number of slaves. On one occasion every soldier in Gragn's army is said to have come into possession of at least 200 mules and slaves and on another men handed around captured gold by the fistful: one man who presented one of his companions with a gift of 50 ounces had it angrily rejected as a mere trifle.

The prosperity produced by such loot came to a sudden end in 1543 when Portugal intervened in support of the Christian ruler, Emperor

Below: Weirdly-coloured windows illuminate the interior of the rickety wooden house built by the eccentric French poet, Rimbaud, during his stay in the ancient city of Harar. The ceiling is covered in painted animal skins depicting pastoral scenes.

Galawdewos, after which Gragn was speedily defeated and killed. Power was then assumed by the defeated leader's widow, Bati Del Wambara, who married her late husband's nephew Nur ibn al-Wazir Mujahid. Together they continued the war which was at times very fierce, the Emperor's army, according to some accounts, actually penetrating the city. Galawdewos was, however, himself later killed in battle with the Muslims in 1559.

Notwithstanding Nur's victory, the Harari state was greatly weakened by the prolonged fighting, with the result that the neighbouring Oromos, or Gallas as they were then sometimes known, advanced to the very borders of the town. Nur, according to local tradition, thereupon constructed around Harar the defensive wall which remains to this day one of its most distinctive features.

Harar was still an important emirate a century and a half ago — to which period date back our first written descriptions of it. The city at this time issued its own currency and was the principal inland emporium of the Horn of Africa.

The earliest published account of Harar is based on the recollections of Ramyat Allah, an Ethiopian merchant from Shoa. He was interviewed by Lieutenant W C Barker, a British officer in Indian service, who published the trader's remarks on the city in the *Journal of the Royal Geographical Society* of 1842. A decade or so later Barker's compatriot, the famous orientalist Sir Richard Burton, spent 10 brief but memorable days in the settlement, and described this in his two-volume work *First Footsteps in East Africa*.

Harar stood, as for centuries past, in rich, well-watered agricultural land. The latter was "highly cultivated", Ramyat Allah states "for miles around", in some places with the help of irrigation from natural springs. The area produced coffee, for which Harar is still famous, as well as "great quantities" of the mild narcotic *khat* (*Catha edulis*), wheat, millet and other grains and "a variety of fruit and vegetables".

The city was large and populous. The houses were "built very close together", Ramyat Allah explains, and covered an extensive area which, according to Burton's estimate, was "about one mile long by half that

breadth" and took no less than two hours to walk round quickly.

The settlement was surrounded by a strong stone and mud wall, judged by Ramyat Allah to be about four metres high by one metre thick. It was, Burton says, " irregular" in shape, "lately repaired but ignorant of cannon" and "pierced with five large gates, and supported by oval towers of artless construction." These, like the buildings within, were made of "rough stones, the granites and sandstones of the hills", and were held together with clay.

These walls, which were guarded by a small but relatively strong band of musketeers, protected the citizens against attack from the neighbouring population which would otherwise have almost certainly overrun the town. This was graphically explained by Ramyat Allah, who had himself received a spear-wound in the course of fighting on the Amir's behalf. He states that the Harar army, though numerically "insignificant", was, on account of its firearms, "far superior" to those of the neighbouring peoples who had "a great dread" of such weapons, perhaps not surprisingly for he says they had "not a single matchlock in their possession." The people around Harar, he adds, were "said to be good horsemen, and frequently manage to surprise the Harari when least expected: they have, however, never been able to enter the town; indeed so great is their dread of the matchlockmen, they have never ventured to attack it".

Further to protect the security of the town, strangers were forbidden to enter the gates without first surrendering their arms. These had to be lodged, Ramyat Allah states, with the Amir, and would not be returned until their owners had safely departed. The gates, Burton confirms, were "at all times . . . carefully guarded", and in the evening the keys were taken to the Amir, after which no one could enter or leave the city until dawn.

The five gates, known in the Harari language as *bari*, were each used by caravans travelling to and from a different area, and each had a specific name.

The chief building within the walls was the great mosque, known as al-Jami. Burton, familiar with finer structures elsewhere in the Middle East, describes it, somewhat patronisingly, as "a large barn of poverty-stricken appearance, with broken-down gates, and two whitewashed minarets of truncated conoid shape". The latter had been built by Turkish architects from Arabia, but one had lately fallen down and been replaced by an "inferior effort" of local art. Besides this mosque there were also "many" smaller ones, Ramyat Allah testifies, but most, according to Burton, were merely "plain buildings, without minarets."

Much more interesting was the Amir's palace, a two-storey structure, with a reception hall in which the chief received his visitors, one of whom was Burton himself, who recalls that the chamber contained a throne and had a Persian rug on its floor. A small room nearby was occupied by the court treasurer who sat on a "large dais covered with Persian carpets" and was surrounded by six councillors, two of them with turbans, the remainder with bare and shaven heads. Beneath the palace proper was the state prison, described by Burton as a "terrible" place where "the captive is heavily ironed". Of this prison it was said that "he who once enters it lives with unkempt beard and untrimmed nails until the day when death sets him free". Beside this dungeon was an inner sanctum reported to house "large hoards of silver, coffee and ivory", as well as "huge boxes of ancient fashion said to contain dollars".

The dwellings of the citizens at large were, as one would expect, much simpler structures. They were for the most part "double-storeyed" buildings which Burton describes as "long, flat-roofed sheds". Their doors were "composed of a single plank" and had "holes for windows pierced high above the ground".

A large proportion of the citizens were in one way or another involved in trade. Ramyat Allah spoke of Harar as "a great commercial town", while Burton called it "the great 'halfway house' for slaves" from the interior. Commercial caravans came and went, the Ethiopian trader states, "at all times". Merchants travelling to the coast carried with them coffee, millet, ghee, ostrich feathers, and saffron, as well as slaves. Such traders brought back in return blue and white coarse cloths, American sheeting, Indian piece goods and European prints, besides silks and shawls, silk thread and red cotton yarn, beads, coral and trinkets, zinc and copper wire, frankincense and gum as well as rice, dates, sugar and gunpowder.

The city was also renowned for its handicrafts, and in particular for its *tobes*, or togas, and sashes which, Burton says, far surpassed "in beauty and durability" the "rapid produce" of European factories. The book-binders of Harar were likewise so accomplished that the discerning orientalist could not "but admire" their bindings, for he was convinced that "no Eastern country save Persia" surpassed them "in strength and appearance".

Harar, for so long a great centre of commerce, in the 1870s attracted the expansionist ambitions of Egypt, which was then ruled by Khedive Ismail. Egyptian forces advancing inland from the port of Zeila seized the city in October 1875, and a few days later the Amir, Abd al-Shakur, was killed by an Egyptian *bashibazuk*, or irregular soldier. The Egyptian occupation encountered strong opposition from the population around the city who on one occasion assembled an army of no fewer than 35,000 men and tried to starve the invaders into submission. The Khedival Government was obliged to increase its garrison which soon reached around 3,500 men, or about a fifth of the male population within the walls. There were constant disputes between occupiers and occupied, though not a few Egyptian officers married Harari girls, in some cases to gain title deeds to the rich agricultural land around the city.

The Egyptians, who were deeply concerned with questions of security, rebuilt the old city walls and parapets and constructed an entirely new fort on an isolated hill to the north-west where they installed two Krupp guns. A new hospital and grain store were also erected, as well as many new stone buildings, a large proportion of them for Egyptian officers.

The Egyptian occupation of Harar, like that of Massawa and other parts of East Africa, came to an end as a consequence of Britain's seizure of Egypt in 1882, the rise of the Sudanese Mahdi, and the British Government's desire to impose retrenchment on the Khedive by liquidating his then only recently established African empire.

These developments produced a crisis in Egypt which was felt at Harar early in 1884, when Khedival payments to the troops ceased and Egyptian soldiers began looting surrounding areas in search of food. Rebellion broke out in the countryside and the city's communications with the coast were interrupted. The British Government shortly afterwards sent two officers to supervise the Egyptian withdrawal from the area. Harar was temporarily under the control of the British, who however soon withdrew. Before doing so they handed over power to a new Amir, Abd Allahi, who sought to re-establish a medieval-type theocratic city state. Staunchly anti-foreign, he allowed the revival of the slave trade which the Egyptians had sought to ban.

The Egyptian withdrawal coincided with Emperor Menilek's reassertion of Ethiopia's greatness. Realising the necessity of re-establishing Ethiopian control over Harar, the Ethiopian ruler informed King Umberto of Italy in June 1885 of his intention of occupying Harar, and declared: "We have no intention of looting and destroying. After taking Harar, we will protect and govern everyone according to his religion. We will subdue and pacify the route from Shoa to the sea. That is what we intend to do."

Towards the end of 1886 Menilek accordingly marched towards Harar. He tried to persuade Amir Abd Allahi to accept his suzerainty without a fight, as other local rulers had done and would soon do, but the chief proved obdurate. A trial of strength took place on 6 January 1887, Ethiopian Christmas Eve, when the Amir sought to surprise Menilek's army. The Harari chief was, however, easily defeated at the battle of Chalanqo. The Harari elders thereupon surrendered. Menilek duly

entered the city and shortly afterwards appointed his cousin, Ras Makonnen, as Governor. Anxious to avoid sectarian strife, Menilek nevertheless entrusted the local administration to the former Amir's nephew Ali, who had previously been imprisoned by his uncle, and issued a decree stating that the citizens, whatever their faith, should thenceforth live in accordance with their religious traditions and beliefs.

The first years of Menilek's occupation were by no means easy, but the city soon began to benefit from its integration in the wider Ethiopian state. Decio Wolynsky, an Italian traveller, reported early in the 20th century that the various inhabitants of Harar "lived in harmony under the protecting shade of the Ethiopian flag", while his compatriot, Captain E A d'Albertis, observed in 1906 that mosque and church stood fraternally side by side, the call of the muezzin and the ringing of church bells alternating peacefully.

Harar flourished economically in the years which followed, the more so as its customs post charged a tax of only eight per cent as against 10 per cent collected in Addis Ababa. Since dues could be paid at either place, "the majority of merchants", as Powell-Cotton notes, preferred to do so at Harar, with the result that "the bulk" of Shoa's trade passed through the city. Exports consisted primarily of coffee, skins and wax, besides durra, saffron, gold, civet, ivory and gum arabic. Imports included cotton, silk and other types of cloth, and glassware, as well as leather, liquors, tools and other metal goods, perfumes, iron, tin, lead and, of major importance, fire-arms.

Traders operating at Harar in this period included persons of many nationalities, among them Frenchmen, Italians, Armenians, Greeks and, later increasingly important, Indians. The best-known foreigner to reside in the city was, however, the renowned French poet, Arthur Rimbaud, who spent the last years of his life supplying Menilek with rifles, and whose remarkable house, adorned with windows of coloured glass, still stands on high ground at the centre of the city overlooking the market.

This period witnessed a considerable amount of building, both governmental and private. In 1902 Ras Makonnen founded a hospital which still bears his name. It was designed by a French architect, M Chatillon, and consisted of a two-storey structure of nine wards. A leprosarium, with one large building and 49 huts, was established in the same year, on the initiative of a French Capuchin missionary, Monseigneur Jarousseau. The missionaries associated with this institution founded Ethiopia's first newspaper, the *Bulletin de la Leproserie de Harar*, which was edited by Father Marie Bernard. Originally duplicated, it began to be printed in 1905 when it changed its name to *Le Semeur d'Ethiopie*. Other innovations of the time included a modern school, set up at Menilek's request by Egyptian Copts in 1906, and in the same year a branch of the Bank of Abyssinia, later to be renamed the Bank of Ethiopia.

Harar was also the first Ethiopian town to possess an hotel. This building was run at the turn of the century by a Frenchman, but was later taken over by other proprietors, at one time Italian and at another Greek. The British traveller Herbert Vivian, one of its early patrons, was much impressed with it. Seeing "a number of Europeans . . . congregated round a billiard table with absinthe at their elbows", he was casually asked by the owner when he would like his shower, and comments, ethnocentrically, that he found himself in an atmosphere "very like civilisation".

Other modern institutions established during the Menilek period included a post, telegraph and telephone office and a prison.

The development of the city was, however, gradually arrested as a consequence of the establishment of the Addis Ababa-Djibouti railway which, for technical reasons, bypassed Harar. Commerce tended as a

180

result to be increasingly diverted to the nearby railway town of Dire Dawa which was known for a time as 'Addis Harar', or 'New Harar'. Despite this setback, however, the old city remained a major political, economic and cultural centre. Many new buildings, including an imposing palace just outside the city walls, several schools and a second hospital, were erected in the inter-war years, as well as further structures during the subsequent Italian occupation. Such developments, however, for the most part taking place outside the walls, scarcely affected the basic character of the city, which retains much of the charm as well as, for its inhabitants, some of the squalor of a medieval walled city.

Harar today, with its atmosphere of history and of past glory amidst the ebb and flow of conquering armies, is thus a fascinating stopping place for the traveller. Its ethnically complex population is made up of Adaris, the indigenous highland Ethiopian people of this region (speaking a Semitic language related to Amharic), Arabs, Oromos and Somali-speakers from the plains. This cultural diversity is best seen expressed in the old market at the centre of the city where tall, graceful

Opposite: Brightly dressed girl of Dire Dawa expresses the cheerful atmosphere of this colourful, flamboyant town.

maidens in long, flowing, extravagantly coloured dresses come to barter and to buy amongst the elegant Moorish archways — a scene that has changed little since the eccentric French poet, Rimbaud, watched it from his equally eccentric house of wood and glass that stands above the commercial area. Famous for its intricately-worked filigree jewellery of silver, gold and amber, Harar's Megala Gudo market is also a centre for the purchase of beautiful baskets of woven, brightly coloured grasses, decorative wall mats and bright shawls, as well as the fruits, vegetables, spices and grains of the province. Outwards from the market twists a warren of steep narrow cobbled alleyways between ancient balconied houses where the traveller may wander until he reaches one of the five gates in the city wall.

Harar's Islamic character is best expressed in the Grand Mosque which dominates the town. Though indeed not large, nor elaborate by Middle Eastern standards, Burton's 19th century description of it as a "poverty-stricken" barn was unkind and inaccurate. Built on 16th-century foundations, its tall whitewashed minarets soar skywards above a broad courtyard in which pilgrims cleanse themselves. The cool spacious interior, dimly illuminated by shafts of sunlight entering through open windows, is filled with the whisper of prayer and click of rosary beads as worshippers recount the 99 names of God.

Near the mosque, as much a symbol of the mutual tolerance of differing faiths in Ethiopia today as it was when Captain d'Albertis observed it in 1906, stands the imposing octagonal Christian cathedral of Medhane Alem built by Emperor Menilek when he captured the city in 1887.

One of the sights of Harar is provided by the famous 'Hyena men' who, as evening falls, set themselves up at points along the outskirts of the city. These men make their living by laying on a remarkable show, throwing meat, offal and bones to packs of wild hyenas that come down from the surrounding hills, apparently answering to names which the Hyena men chant hypnotically . . . *Debebe, Taferra, Umar.* One by one, they appear out of the darkness, their eyes glowing and jaws slavering savagely. The few dollars each that the watchers are expected to pay are a small price indeed for the privilege of being party to so bizarre a spectacle. As the hyenas dart forward to snatch up the scraps, fights break out amongst them and their throaty snarls mingle with eerie demented giggles in an elemental cacophony of sound.

An interesting excursion from Harar takes the traveller on a gravel road that runs eastwards towards the Somali border. Offering attractive views of the city which, in some lights, looks more like an idealised artistic impression of Bethlehem than a medieval fortress of African

Islam, this road soon leaves all signs of civilisation behind as it winds up scrub-covered hillsides and cuts through narrow passes. Midway between Harar and the town of Jigjiga, near the eastern edge of the escarpment, a deep valley is entered, known locally as 'the Valley of Marvels' — an area of unusual volcanic formations where tall columns of black rock, withered and twisted by the elements, stand topped by loose, precariously-balanced boulders. Here the Somali-speaking nomads of this region bring camels in their thousands to graze on the thorn bushes and thin grass. Fierce men armed with long curved knives and with spears, and statuesque women bearing wooden milk containers strapped to their backs, they seem totally at home in this strange, ethereal landscape.

Westwards, and somewhat to the north of Harar, at an altitude of 1,200 metres, stands the town of Dire Dawa which, in the early years of this century, first began to rise to prominence as a staging post on the railway connecting the port of Djibouti with the Ethiopian capital Addis Ababa. The line reached Dire Dawa in 1902. Immediately, much of the rich trade that had previously passed through Harar began to be diverted here, and many merchants moved from the older to the newer settlement.

From the date that the railway arrived in Dire Dawa, the town began to develop as two adjacent but distinct settlements. One was established by the railway company, party for its own staff, while the other sprang up more or less spontaneously around the market. These two clearly defined centres are very much part of the character of the town today. They are separated by the Dechatu stream which is for most of the year no more than a dry bed, but during the rains flushes into a fast-flowing torrent.

The railway town, which lies to the north and west of the Dechatu, was planned and largely constructed by the engineers, mainly but not exclusively French, responsible for the construction of the railway. This settlement developed with remarkable rapidity. An American envoy, Robert Skinner, described it in 1903, only one year after its establishment, as already a "boom city", while the Italian observer, Dr Decio Wolynsky, noted in the following year that most of the railway company's buildings had risen in less than a 12-month. They included not only the station itself, but also a number of warehouses and workshops, as well as numerous dwellings for company personnel.

The section of the town differed from most other Ethiopian settlements in that it was constructed in a carefully thought-out manner, with straight roads and well aligned buildings. It was also unusual in having piped water, which came from two nearby natural springs. There were also exceptionally numerous flowers and bushes which made the place, as Wolynsky exclaimed, a "gracious city". Dire Dawa's trade, which in the early days was largely in Greek, Armenian and Indian hands, was from the outset considerable, and several of the town's shops had a turnover rivalling that of many establishments in Addis Ababa. This atmosphere of commercial prosperity is still very much apparent, perhaps most particularly in the crowded Afetieissa market which stocks modern goods in great numbers as well as the more traditional produce of eastern Ethiopia. Like the old Muslim market at Harar, Afetieissa is a melting pot for the peoples of the surrounding region, and the Somali, Afar, Oromo and Arab tongues are all spoken here, as well as Amharic, French and not a little English.

In the 'railway town', bright jacarandas and flamboyants line the wide avenues, and horse-drawn buggies provide a cheap taxi service that enables the visitor to make the most of the warm delightful climate that is, undoubtedly, Dire Dawa's most attractive feature. Here the station stands in a broad courtyard surrounded by small shops, and large crowds of people gather, passengers mingling with cigarette and sweet sellers, as the trains pull in with screeching brakes and clanking carriages.

Although the original steam engines have long since been replaced by diesel, the trains running from Dire Dawa to Addis Ababa still have a wild, pioneering atmosphere. The hot, slow journey as the railway descends from the eastern hills, crosses the floor of the Rift Valley and ascends again into the western escarpment, is a unique travel experience, imbued with historical associations. It also affords an opportunity to meet and mingle with ordinary Ethiopians in a way that most other forms of transport deny.

This railway, which plays an extremely important role in the modern Ethiopian economy, carrying a large share of its imports and exports, was first conceived by the Swiss craftsman, Alfred Ilg, who arrived in the country in 1877 to take up the post of technical adviser to Emperor Menilek. Having himself spent no less than seven months on the overland journey from the coast to Addis Ababa, he was fully aware of the inconvenience of mule transport, the high cost of which greatly hampered trade in low-priced commodities, such as coffee, skins and wax, which then constituted the bulk of Ethiopia's exports. Menilek was interested in Ilg's proposal for a railway and in December 1889, wrote to President Carnot of France expressing his desire that a line should be constructed to link the Ethiopian capital with the port of Djibouti in the then French Somaliland Protectorate. This port was favoured because it possessed an excellent harbour and plenty of good water, and was under the control of the French who, unlike the Italians and British, were

*Below: At Awash station food-
vendors board the train on the
Addis Ababa-Djibouti railway,
selling spicy food and snacks to
travellers.*

thought to have no ambitions of penetrating inland. The French
Government however, for a number of reasons, did little to encourage
Menilek and his objective and, after waiting three years, the Emperor
empowered Ilg to establish a private railway company.

After a further year's study and discussion Menilek granted Ilg a
formal concession, in March 1894, for a company, the *Compagnie Impérial
des Chemins de Fers Ethiopiens*, which was to build and operate a line from
Djibouti right across Ethiopia to the White Nile. The line was to be
constructed in three sections: the first from the port of Djibouti to the old
commercial city of Harar, the second from Harar to Entoto (the mountain
settlement above Addis Ababa) which was still considered the Ethiopian
capital, and the third from Entoto to the White Nile. The company was to
be allowed a 99-year monopoly for each stretch of line dating from its
completion. Ilg and the French merchant, Léon Chefneux, who became
his partner at about this time, soon afterwards obtained Menilek's
permission for the concession to be modified so that the line could be
diverted from the Harar mountains, where construction costs would

have been considerable, to the nearby valley of Dire Dawa. The company later obtained agreement from the French Minister of the Colonies in March 1897 for the railway to run across French Protectorate territory.

Construction work began in Djibouti in October 1897. The first task was the erection of the railway station, offices, workshops and storage sheds, as well as dwellings and other amenities for railway and construction staff. French Protectorate authorities at the same time took steps to improve the Djibouti harbour, by building a breakwater and no fewer than five lighthouses.

Steps were then taken to begin laying the railway line. To minimise cost, a narrow-gauge of only one metre was adopted, but expensive iron sleepers, popularly known in the French iron trade as 'Menileks', had to be used in view of the presence of termites which could be expected to consume anything made of wood.

For every kilometre of line, over 70 tons of rails, sleepers and telegraph poles had to be transported, not to mention sand, cement, water and provisions for the workers. A huge force of camels was soon journeying backwards and forwards transporting such supplies. Another source of expense arose from difficulties of terrain. Two large viaducts and many smaller earthworks had to be built within the first 50 or so kilometres of line, and others further inland. Anti-French interests were, moreover, actively stirring up popular opposition to the line, thus necessitating the employment of numerous guards, while many of the local tribesmen, in need of metal for their spearheads and bangles, developed a passion for hacking up railway lines and tearing down the company's telegraph wire.

The cost of constructing the railway soon proved much higher than originally budgeted for. The company in consequence ran into financial difficulties even before the line reached Ethiopian territory. Ilg and Chefneux were obliged to turn to British entrepreneurs for help and these and other investors established a holding company. British investment was bitterly opposed in France and there was a violent outcry in the autumn of 1901 to the effect that French interests had been betrayed by the company and that rapacious England was seeking to supplant France in an enterprise initiated by French foresight and capital. The French Government duly responded to this agitation. The Governor of the French Somaliland Protectorate, M Bonhoure, was accordingly authorised to conclude a new Convention with Chefneux, in February 1902. This document, which ignored the concession earlier granted by Menilek, provided the company with a subsidy of 500,000 francs payable over 50 years. In return Chefneux, who had by then gained control of the company, agreed that it should be bound hand

and foot to France, and that the French Government could in certain circumstances even take over parts of the line in Ethiopian territory.

This Convention, which violated his original concession and infringed Ethiopian sovereignty, greatly angered Menilek, the more so as he had not been consulted about its provisions and had learnt about it only through the British representative in Addis Ababa who sought to inflame his mind against it. The result was that the Emperor refused to cooperate with the company, and did nothing, as had been previously hoped, to encourage merchants to abandon their camels and mules and to turn instead to the railway. He refused, moreover, to give the company permission to start work on the second stretch of line from Dire Dawa to the capital. This refusal had a serious effect on investment, for would-be shareholders realised that profits could not be expected until the railway reached the Ethiopian capital.

The company was soon in great financial difficulty. To complete the line as far as Dire Dawa it was obliged to cede its subsidy, which would have brought in 25 million francs over 50 years, for 11.3 million francs. This desperate measure enabled the proprietors of the company to repay 3,000,000 francs borrowed from the British. By the summer of 1904 the company was, however, on the verge of bankruptcy. Unable to extend the line inland beyond Dire Dawa it was losing money heavily every month, and found itself obliged once more to turn for help to the British, who, desirous of modifying the French character of the railway, began to propose its "internationalisation". This idea also received support from French chambers of commerce who regarded it as the sole way of breaking the impasse resulting from the Bonhoure-Chefneux Convention.

Menilek at this point dramatically resumed the initiative over the railway. In April 1905 he summoned the envoys of the four Great Powers represented at his court, France, Britain, Italy and Russia. He reminded them that for "several years" he had pursued the task of endowing the country with a railway, but that for the previous three years work had stopped and time had been "wasted on idle discussions". Emphasising that the coming of the line would have "contributed to the development of the country", which was his "principal preoccupation", he appealed to the four Governments to submit proposals that would reconcile their several interests, but warned that if they failed to do so he would be obliged to undertake the construction himself.

The Powers failed, however, to come to any agreement over the internationalisation of the line, and in the spring of 1906 Menilek therefore began clearing a track from Addis Ababa towards Dire Dawa prior to the actual laying of the line. The British, French and Italians

188

Below: A child perches on the branches of a tree above Bishofu crater-lake at Debre Zeit. A recreational centre less than one hour's drive from Addis Ababa, Debre Zeit is an attractive and fast developing town. Its series of lovely lakes hints at the volcanic past of the region.

responded in December by signing a Tripartite Convention 'dividing' Ethiopia between them into three spheres of influence. By this agreement the British and Italians recognised that any railway between Dire Dawa and Addis Ababa should belong to France, while the French Government agreed that the line should extend no further than Addis Ababa, for the lands to the west of the capital were to fall within the British and Italian spheres of influence. Menilek, on learning of this Convention, thanked the Powers for notifying him of it, but proudly declared that it could not bind him in his decisions.

The Tripartite Convention spelled an end to hopes of internationalising the railway. The French Government thereupon ordered the company to repay its debts to the British and, since this was impossible, forced it into bankruptcy, with the result that it was officially liquidated in January 1908.

The liquidation of the company brought about a fortunate end to the conflict, as well as an opportunity for the various parties to start afresh, save face and learn from past mistakes. Menilek, confronted with the Tripartite Convention of 1906, saw that he could not hope to internationalise the railway, but had to resign himself to a French line, the alternative of constructing it himself being apparently unsatisfactory if not impracticable. He was, however, able to issue a new and more carefully worded concession in January 1908, designed to safeguard himself against the kind of untoward developments which had resulted in the 1902 Convention. The French likewise profited from experience and took care to give the Emperor no further affront.

Menilek's new concession, which was once more granted for a 99-year period, was made out to the Emperor's personal physician, Dr Vitalien, a coloured man from Guadeloupe. The principle that the railway was to be owned privately rather than by a foreign government was thus reaffirmed. It was, however, recognised from the outset that Vitalien was merely a "man of straw" and that the company would be under the control of a French bank, the Banque de l'Indochine, which because of its wealth would be able to shoulder the considerable expenditure required to complete the line.

A new railway company was duly established in March 1908 and construction was soon resumed. Despite the difficulties of the terrain, the need to transport supplies over immense distances, and political problems in the aftermath of Menilek's death, the line was extended to Akaki, 23 kilometres from Addis Ababa, by 1915, and eventually reached the capital two years later.

The railway thus came into full operation in 1917, a full 20 years after the beginning of construction work at Djibouti. The service, which has operated ever since, traverses a line of 785 kilometres: 311 kilometres from the port to Dire Dawa; 237 kilometres from Dire Dawa to Awash station; and 237 kilometres from Awash to the capital. The line has 29 tunnels, one of them nearly 100 metres long, and 34 stations, as well as hotels at Dire Dawa and Awash, and restaurants at Aisha, Afdem, Mieso and Mojjo.

Probably the most colourful station of the whole line is Awash, at the heart of the Ethiopian Rift Valley, 860 metres above sea-level and 225 kilometres to the east of Addis Ababa. Here, from the tree-lined, flower-strewn gardens of an excellent restaurant serving both Ethiopian and Italian food, the traveller may view the ceaseless life of the railway as the crowds of passengers and well-wishers flood out to surround the incoming trains in a hubbub of excitement. Food sellers and cigarette vendors stroll past the open windows of the carriages offering their wares, and bundles of *khat*, the leafy stimulant chewed throughout eastern Ethiopia, are taken on board.

Awash station stands at the eastern end of the Awash National Park, where dik-dik, waterbuck, ostrich, gazelle, zebra, oryx and other plains game can be seen in great numbers, as well as some cheetahs and leopards. The great Awash River flows through the park, descending thunderously over a steep waterfall, and thence follows a winding course across the floor of a 700-metre-deep gorge, overlooked by the lodges of the Ras Hotel.

This is a volcanic region, dominated by the still active cone of Mount Fantalle. Layers of broken basalt betray older seismic activity and everywhere steaming fumaroles remind the visitor of the continuing tumult that rages beneath the thin earth. On the north side of the park, an extensive area of hot-springs lies like a great oasis surrounded by tall green doum palms amidst a dry desert of scrub and thorn trees. Emerging from several deep sources, the super-heated water quickly cools to temperatures that swimmers can tolerate and spreads out in widening pools of translucent turquoise. Long fan-like clusters of doum fronds overhang the water, with a few graceful trunks bowing down to form convenient hammocks and seats. The doums, too, obscure the worst heat of the sun so that only a cool and dappled green light filters through. A soft breeze blows constantly, rustling the palms, producing a gentle sibilation. This is a place of peace and quiet for the soul and of healing vapours for the body, that rests and refreshes the traveller, cleansing him of weariness and of the dust of the road.

The hot-springs of the Awash National Park are only a part of the long series of spas and therapeutic bathing places that the volcanic heritage of the Rift has enabled Ethiopia to establish. At Sodere, 120

Right: In the heart of the Awash National Park graceful doum palms surround a natural hot-spring that wells up to fill a deep pool. The translucent waters are reputed to have therapeutic properties.

kilometres to the south-west, a major new hotel complex, with two large modern swimming pools, has grown up amidst extensive orchards and flower gardens on the site of a tradition spa which has been described as the 'Lourdes of Africa' because of the marvellous curative and rejuvenatory properties of its sulphurous waters. There are hot-springs at Nazareth, too, just 90 kilometres from Addis Ababa, and at Debre Zeit a series of crater lakes which speak of the great volcanic outpourings that did so much to mould the topography and character of this whole region. Even the capital itself, high above the Rift at an altitude of 2,400 metres, has its share of developed spas — indeed, the land on which Addis Ababa is built was called 'Filwoha' (the Amharic word for hot-spring) before Emperor Menilek moved his entourage here in the 19th century. However, of all the hot-springs in Ethiopia, the palm-lined pools in the Awash National Park, as yet wholly uncommercialised, remain the most beautiful — a beauty enhanced by their savage natural surroundings and by the thousands of birds — egrets, cormorants and cranes, plovers, geese and pelicans — that come to feed amongst their pristine reed bed.

Northwards from Awash station, a fine macadamised road leads out of the national park and points arrow-straight across sere low-lying plains to Eritrea's far-away Red Sea port of Assab. Following this road into the widening triangle of the Great Rift Valley, the traveller passes through ever hotter and drier terrain, but remains tantalisingly aware of the cool and airy heights of the escarpment that loom up to the west, blue and distant across the shimmering desert.

The relationship between the nomadic warriors of the Rift and the farming peoples of the nearby highlands was long an uneasy one, with the result that when the centre of power in medieval Ethiopia shifted from Axum and Lalibela further south to Shoa the emperors of the time often made their military capitals on vantage points at the edge of the escarpment overlooking the Valley. One of the first of such capitals was established in the mid-15th century at Debre Birhan, 133 kilometres north of Addis Ababa, at a height of 2,840 metres. Its founder was the great Emperor Zara Yaqob, a man who spent most of his life on campaign.

The establishment of Debre Birhan is recorded in the royal chronicle of this reign, which, following the practice of old-time writers, gives it a supernatural setting by claiming that a mysterious light suddenly appeared in the sky above the site of the future settlement.

The story of this heavenly light is also preserved in another Ethiopian work of this period, the *Ta'amra Maryam*, or Miracles of Mary, which states that a "great light" appeared in and around the King's camp, over the nearby churches where it "illuminated curtains and vestments", and above the tents of the soldiers whose clothes were lit up, as a result of which there was "great joy". The remarkable illumination is said to have remained visible for "several days" and "seemed like a flame of fire, but did not burn". It brightened the face of anyone who approached, and gladdened the heart. A group of monks who witnessed the sight from afar are reported to have wondered whether the King's palace was in flames, on which account they grieved greatly for "the light seemed like a terrestrial flame".

Zara Yaqob, the chronicle claims, was so moved by this luminous vision that he decided to build a palace on the site, and called it Debre Birhan, or 'Place of Light'. A church was also built here, Debre Birhan Sellassie, which stands to this day though the palace has long since disappeared.

The illumination so vividly described in these and other early Ethiopian legends does not seem to require any supernatural explanation. The light was almost certainly produced by Halley's Comet which appeared in 1456 and, according to recent computer estimates, would have been seen in Shoa around sunset and sunrise, from 8 May to 27 July, during which period it would have blazed a fiery trail across a large stretch of the Ethiopian sky.

Zara Yaqob, according to the chronicle, spent the rest of his reign at Debre Birhan. After his death in 1468, however, his son and successor Baeda Maryam transferred his capital to another site, as a result of which the city lost much of its importance and sank for several centuries into near oblivion. The old capital, however, acquired new prominence in the early 18th century as a result of the rise of Nagasi, founder of the later Shoan dynasty, who established his headquarters on the site of the earlier settlement, the remains of which were no doubt then still in existence. He and his successors made use, however, of several other capitals. King Sahle Sellassie, who received envoys from Britain and France in the 1840s, thus spent only a fraction of his time in Debre Birhan for he also resided extensively at three nearby settlements, the principal of which was Ankober, a few kilometres to the west.

Ankober, today a small and undistinguished rural town, had exactly the strategic qualities that Sahle Sallassie required since, as was noted by Charles Johnston, a British visitor of the time, it stood "upon a height commanding the only road leading from the low countries to the tableland of Shoa".

The hill of Ankober was dominated, the French travellers Combes and Tamisier state, by the King's palace, a stone and mortar construction with gable ends, "remarkable for its great size". The compound was guarded by spiral lines of wooden palisades which extended from the

base to the summit of the hill, and were "interspersed" another contemporary writer observes, "with barred stockades, between which are profusely scattered the abodes of household slaves, with breweries, kitchens, cellars, storehouses, magazines and granaries". The houses of the principal nobles were studded around the palace on "five distinct knolls", and were "of all sizes and all shapes". There were many gardens, some with cedars and other large trees. The town had such a pleasing appearance it caused the French envoy, Rochet d'Hericourt, to exclaim that it was "one of the most ravishing amphitheatres" in the world.

Ankober, as a capital town of the mid-19th century, had a large population, much of it in the service of the king. The inhabitants, according to Johnston, thus included "at least 1,000 riflemen, several hundred priests" and over a thousand slaves.

The town, which was also the capital of Sahle Sellassie's son and successor, Haile Melakot, was occupied by Emperor Tewodros' forces in 1855. Before this happened, however, Haile Melakot's officers burnt

Above: On a misty hilltop, in front of the ruined walls of the ancient fortress at Ankober, herdsboys amuse themselves playing Gebeta, *a game of skill popular throughout Ethiopia.*

down the palace and broke all the jars containing their master's mead. This, it is said, produced such a torrent that it swept away the house of the King's door-keeper. Tewodros subsequently erected his tent on the ruins of the palace, and spent a week there, during which time, a contemporary chronicle states, he "examined the various establishments of the town". The capital, because of its great elevation, was then almost wrapped in cloud.

Ankober was further damaged during a rebellion against Tewodros' rule in 1857, but was rebuilt in the late 1870s after Menilek's return to Shoa. The town was shortly afterwards described by a French engineer, Alphonse Aubry, as nestling over two hills, with its main church on a third. By then the "most populous" settlement in Shoa, Ankober had once more several thousand inhabitants, including many palace employees, such as weavers, tailors, blacksmiths, tanners, saddlers, jewellers and makers of musical instruments.

With the establishment of Addis Ababa in the late 19th century, and the rerouting of import-export trade, in part as a result of the railway between the new capital and Djibouti, Ankober lost most of its *raison d'etre*, and appears to the traveller arriving there today to be very much a town of the past. Amidst the ruins of the hilltop palace — which had little permanence despite Menilek's rebuilding — herdsboys play. Ghostly mists often enshroud the broken and crumbling walls, obscuring the view to the plummeting depths of the Rift below.

Two principal roads run northwards through Ethiopia at this point, pursuing roughly parallel courses. The oldest, built by Italian occupying forces during World War II, snakes along the escarpment edge, connecting Addis Ababa to Debre Birhan, bypassing Ankober and proceeding on through the towns of Debre Sina, Robit, Efeson, Senbeta, Chefa and Kombolcha to Dessie, capital of what was Wollo. Less than 100 kilometres to the east, along the floor of the Rift Valley, the main Awash to Assab trunk-route, which was completed in 1973, cuts through the heat and dust of a terrain radically different from that of the cool uplands.

The low road is without doubt the faster of the two but, apart from the diversion provided by the wildlife of the Awash and Danakil National Parks, it is also the less interesting. The high road, which itself at times descends almost to the Rift Valley plains, offers a far more stimulating spectacle of varied scenery and peoples as it cuts into giant tunnels, winds down mountainsides too massive for any engineer to blast through, and then curves up again in tight hairpin bends to the top of the escarpment. South of Debre Sina it enters a land of cloud where children sell fez-shaped woollen caps and blankets to provide protection from the

cold. But north of this pretty alpine town it drops quickly, 500 metres or more, into warmer climes in which mango trees and jacarandas thrive. Here nomadic Oromos and Afars herd their cattle slowly to market at Senbeta, checking in their rifles with the local Government office when they arrive and collecting them again only when they leave. The road rises briefly up a mountainside again beyond Karakore through a eucalyptus belt where the air cools and freshens, then runs northwards along a plateau at 1,800 metres into Kombolcha. From here it jinks suddenly west, rearing up into the Allamatta range, climbing 700 vertical metres over a horizontal distance of 23 kilometres to the town of Dessie. The tiny straight line on the map that represents the section of the road from Kombolcha to Dessie does not do justice to the roller-coaster sweep of bends and steep gradients that the traveller encounters here, or to the truly astounding views of height and depth telescoped together that the road affords.

The sometimes quarrelsome but often productive relationship between highlander and lowlander that has played so great a part in the colourful

Above: Afar women lead their burden camels across a volcanic plain made green by a brief shower of rain. Soon the merciless sun will dry out the land once again and the grass will wither. However, the Afar, used to the caprice of nature, continue the hardy pattern of their lives. A proud, resilient, resourceful people, they have much to teach industrialised man.

Below: Held on Monday mornings, Bati market occupies the slopes of a hill. Grains are sold at the lower levels and camels dominate the peak. A handsome youth, bottom, wearing the long, curved knife of the Afar, inspects livestock at the market.

history of this region finds its modern expression in the town of Bati, 65 kilometres to the east of Dessie. Here, at a mid-point of 1,600 metres above sea-level, the trade of the hills comes down to meet the trade of the plains, and Amharic and Tigrinya speakers from the escarpment mingle with the Oromos and Afars from the Rift Valley.

Bati is the site of Ethiopia's largest cattle and camel market and, indeed — with the exception of Addis Ababa's Mercato — the largest market of any kind in the country.

Held on Monday mornings, starting at dawn and finishing well before noon, it attracts tens of thousands of people, creating an unforgettable spectacle. The market slopes over a low hill crowned with groaning, burbling camels tended by fierce featured Afar men. Lower down hides and skins are sold by dark-eyed women with the proudly beautiful, stately bearing the nomadic life seems to engender. To one side in a fenced enclosure, longhorn cattle are penned awaiting purchasers, while, in the heart of the market, the produce of the highlands is put on sale — chickens, grains, vegetables and spices, shoes, clothing, rope, silver jewellery and manufactured goods. Soap, cooking utensils, cigarettes and tobacco are here laid out amidst bars of rock-salt and measures of sugar, tea and coffee. An assault on the senses, Bati in the memory becomes a kaleidoscope of contrasts — mixed scents of incense, drying skins, cow dung and camels; the mingled sounds of haggling people shouting in a myriad of tongues, the lowing of cattle and the bleat of goats; the visual impact of grains making splashes of yellow and brown, berries — splashes of red, jewellery reflecting in various hues of silver and gold, bright and dull garments, dark and light complexions, patches of sun and patches of shade.

Opposite: Afar girl at Bati, Ethiopia's largest cattle and camel market.

Beyond Bati to the east, on a feeder road that connects the escarpment towns with the main north-south highway running through the Rift Valley from Awash station to Assab, the traveller quickly finds himself once more in a desert environment. East again, as far as the Gulf of Aden and north as far as the Red Sea, this is a land of blackened lava flows and sandy plains strewn with boulders baking under a fierce desiccating heat. Across it flows the great Awash River, attracting life and greenery to its banks, a fragile expression of hope soon defeated — for the Awash fails in its quest to reach the sea. Not far north of the town of Mile it begins to meander and thereafter dissipates its force into a series of shallow pools which soon evaporate. Only in its most powerful floods is the river allowed to add some transitory centimetres to the thick waters of the scattered handful of saline lakes that lie on the borders of Ethiopia and the Republic of Djibouti.

The road, busy with trucks, is the only other source of life in this region, cutting through basalt formations into the mystical amphitheatre of the Dobi desert. Once the bed of a prehistoric ocean, this chaotic landscape glows eerily with the mineral phosphorescence of salt-flats out of which rise dark islands of lava. Giant sandstorms blown on the edge of howling winds obscure the horizon and the sky, and dust-devils dance among the mirages in the shallow bowl of the earth.

A land haunted by *djinis* and hyena spirits, the upper reaches of the Ethiopian Rift speak eloquently to the traveller of the dawn of our world. Ribs and vertebrae of extinct volcanoes protrude everywhere out of the parched ground, and it is not difficult to imagine the smoke, fire and brimstone that once belched forth from the crumbling mouths of the crater rims. This was the land of Dinqinesh, our remote, distant, more than three million-year-old ancestor, the land in which the human species was born. The visitor here today cannot help but reflect on the debt that we owe to her and to her kind in their struggle to survive, to evolve and to grow against the implacable will of the elements.

Miraculously, human life still persists here. Around the site at Hadar

where Donald Johanson discovered the fossilised bones of *Austalopithecus afarensis*, and over a vast expanse of the most hostile terrain that the Rift Valley has to offer, resilient nomads wander with their cattle, camels and goats. It was in honour of these remarkable people, the Afar, that Johanson coined for Dinqinesh her scientific name. Naturally shy of all strangers, but ready to offer friendship and warmth once their suspicions are allayed, they have, in their simple, austere lifestyle, much to teach industrialised man. Sparing, careful use of the resources at their disposal, ingenuity in overcoming the challenges of nature, courage in the face of adversity, an indomitable will that refuses to accept defeat or humiliation, a soaring restless spirit that ever seeks for greener pastures — these are the central values of their culture, values which, in their wider context, have made the human race masters of the earth, sea and skies, values which, for all our modern complacency, we forget at our peril.